teach® yourself

classical music
stephen collins

For over 60 years, more than 40 million people have learnt over 750 subjects the **teach yourself** way, with impressive results.

be where you want to be
with **teach yourself**

D0337105

I would like to thank Terry Sutcliffe for guiding me through a perplexing range of clarinets, past and present. Thanks also to the Teach Yourself editorial team, and especially to Catherine Coe, for her patience, understanding and resourcefulness in putting this book together.

ABERDEENSHIRE LIBRARY AND INFORMATION SERVICE	
1680127	
CAW	342366
781.68	£14.99
	PORP

For UK order enquiries: please contact Bookpoint Ltd.,
130 Milton Park, Abingdon, Oxon OX14 4SB.
Telephone: +44 (0) 1235 827720. Fax: +44 (0) 1235 400454.
Lines are open 09.00–18.00, Monday to Saturday,
with a 24-hour message answering service.
You can also order through our website www.madaboutbooks.com.

For USA order enquiries: please contact
McGraw-Hill Customer Services, PO Box 545, Blacklick,
OH 43004-0545, USA.
Telephone: 1-800-722-4726. Fax: 1-614-755-5645.

For Canada order enquiries: please contact
McGraw-Hill Ryerson Ltd., 300 Water St, Whitby,
Ontario L1N 9B6, Canada.
Telephone: 905 430 5000. Fax: 905 430 5020.

Long renowned as the authoritative source for self-guided learning – with more than 30 million copies sold worldwide – the *Teach Yourself* series includes over 300 titles in the fields of languages, crafts, hobbies, business, computing and education.

British Library Cataloguing in Publication Data
a catalogue record for this title is available from The British Library

Library of Congress Catalog Card Number: On file

First published in UK 2003 by Hodder Headline Ltd.,
338 Euston Road, London, NW1 3BH.

First published in US 2003 by Contemporary Books,
a Division of The McGraw-Hill Companies,
1 Prudential Plaza, 130 East Randolph Street,
Chicago, IL 60601 USA.

The 'Teach Yourself' name is a registered trade mark of
Hodder & Stoughton Ltd.

Copyright © 1997, 2003 Steve Collins

In UK: All rights reserved. No part of this publication may be reproduced or transmitted in any form or by any means, electronic or mechanical, including photocopy, recording, or any information storage and retrieval system, without permission in writing from the publisher or under licence from the Copyright Licensing Agency Limited. Further details of such licences (for reprographic reproduction) may be obtained from the Copyright Licensing Agency Limited, of 90 Tottenham Court Road, London W1T 4LP.

In US: All rights reserved. Except as permitted under the United States Copyright Act of 1976, no part of this publication may be reproduced or distributed in any form or by any means, or stored in a database or retrieval system, without the prior written permission of Contemporary Books.

Composer illustrations from Corbis.
Typeset by Dorchester Typesetting Group Ltd, Dorchester, Dorset.
Printed in Great Britain for Hodder & Stoughton Educational,
a division of Hodder Headline Ltd., 338 Euston Road, London
NW1 3BH by J.W. Arrowsmiths, Bristol.

Impression number   10 9 8 7 6 5 4 3 2 1
Year   2009 2008 2007 2006 2005 2004 2003

contents

There have been several important changes to the new edition of *Teach Yourself Classical Music*.

- The book has been completely revised and updated, with new material added.

- The format is now larger, with photographs as well as line drawings.

- We are fortunate to have a CD (courtesy of Naxos, Britain's leading classical CD label) with excellent performances of some of the main pieces that are discussed in the book. As I mention in Chapter 01, writing and talking about music creates difficulties in finding mutually understood descriptions of what is essentially an aural and sensual experience. This is not to say that words are useless in connection with music, only that they cannot convey precisely the sounds we hear. Far better to have a first-rate performance to experience, then the words can be provide a guide and conduit to a greater understanding and appreciation of the wonderful sounds we can hear.

About the CD

On our CD, we have the following pieces, which I chose carefully to lead the newcomer gently into the world of classical music, and to develop in power and intensity (and length) as we go along, although each step is carefully signposted and the progression is, I hope, always smooth and logical. It would have been impossible in the length of a CD to cover all styles and periods of music that are described in the book, and a strict chronology is not always observed. Instead the pieces follow the rationale of the chapters in the first half of the book, which is explained in the Introduction. The works are not all subjected to rigorous technical analysis (no written music is used); sometimes we look at the construction, other times the emotional and dramatic impact. Here is a list of the works you will hear, and a brief description of each:

Track 1: Haydn, Symphony No. 94, 'The Surprise', 2nd movement
This is the simplest tune imaginable, but Haydn the alchemist transmutes base metal into gold. The orchestra is Capella Istropolitana, conducted by Barry Wordsworth.

Track 2: Haydn, Symphony No. 94, 'The Surprise', 3rd movement
There is a rustic feel to this minuet, with a very strong waltz-like rhythm. I imagine a country house dance, with Mr D'Arcy and Elizabeth Bennett exchanging acerbic remarks as the dancers meet, and part in accordance with the strict formalities of the dancing.

Track 3: Mozart, Symphony No. 40, 1st movement
One of the greatest works by this most gifted of composers, we look quite closely at the structure of this movement, with its deceptively simple melodies, and perfection of form. Played here with great attack and gusto by the Capella Istropolitana, under Barry Wordsworth.

Track 4: Mendelssohn, *Hebrides* overture, 'Fingal's Cave'
This is the first of our two sea voyages, and we encounter

a storm on the way over to the Isle of Staffa to see Fingal's Cave. Performed by the Slovak Philharmonic Orchestra, conducted by Oliver Dohnányi.

Track 5: Beethoven, Symphony No. 6 'Pastoral'

The composer's title for this movement, 'Awakening of Happy Feelings on Arriving in the Countryside' describes the rural scene where Beethoven came to terms with the tragedy of his deafness. The Nicolaus Esterházy Sinfonia, conducted by Béla Drahos, is heard on this recording.

Track 6: Debussy, 'Jeux de Vagues' from *La Mer*

Here we have an impressionistic seascape, painted by a master, using a new orchestral pallet. This bright recording observes all the delicate nuances of the piece, even the tiniest pinpoints of light from the triangle, at the top of the orchestral mix. It is performed for us by Alexander Rahbari, conducting the BRT Philharmonic Orchestra, Brussels.

Tracks 7 and 8: Berlioz, *Symphonie Fantastique* – 'March to the Scaffold' and 'The Witches' Sabbath'

A grisly execution scene is portrayed first, in the fevered imagination of a drug-crazed artist, followed by a wild debauch in the Witches' Sabbath. There is a particularly spooky owl in this recording, played on the flute, with a splendid fall at the end of a long note, clearly intoning 'to woo!' The whole story is revealed in Chapter 06. The orchestra here is the Slovak Radio Symphony Orchestra, under Pinchas Steinberg.

Track 9: Wagner, 'Siegfried's Rhine Journey' from *Götterdämmerung*

Beginning with a whisper, the orchestra demonstrates its huge dynamic range as the doomed hero makes his final journey. The vast legend, which Wagner tells over four nights of musical drama, is also outlined in Chapter 06. Uwe Mund conducts the Slovak Radio Symphony Orchestra in this final piece.

▶ Throughout the book, this symbol indicates when the piece described is on the CD.

I hope you enjoy listening to the music on this CD as much as I have. In addition to these works, there are other examples described in the course of this book. They are not on our CD, but recordings of all are widely available, and I do recommend that you buy some of them if you possibly can. They would form the foundation of your collection, to give you many hours of enjoyment as you explore the world of classical music.

The glossary

As you go along, you will inevitably encounter some musical terminology, which may be unfamiliar. It is one of the aims of this book to clarify and explain these terms so that you can feel confident about your understanding of them. So, when you come across a word in **bold** type, you will find a definition of that word in the glossary at the back of the book.

part one

understanding classical music

The world of classical music is expanding all the time. Boundaries are being broken down, and the old narrow definitions of the music are no longer adequate. Similarly, the audience is widening – 50 years ago, classical music was considered to be accessible only to a cultured elite, who were familiar through their background and education with the conventions and repertoire of this type of music. Classical music was considered 'high brow', and supposedly the antithesis of 'popular' forms enjoyed by the masses of 'ordinary' people who made up the majority of the population of most western countries.

Happily, this kind of snobbery has now largely disappeared, and many more people are keen to enjoy classical music through recordings, radio and television, as well as live performances. All of these media are discussed in the forthcoming pages, but before we begin, some fundamental questions have to be asked about what is, after all, a rich and varied musical palette. The purpose of this book is to demystify and help to open up this type of music to the newcomer, but not to oversimplify the music. The enormous variety and historical significance of this musical world means that a certain amount of effort must be made by the listener to familiarize him/herself with the various forms and practices that are associated with classical music. If no effort were necessary, then the experience would not be particularly rewarding and there would be no need for this book.

A word about written music (notation)

First of all, please be reassured that you don't have to be able to read music to get the most out of this book. I have not used any formal musical notation when describing the sounds of the pieces discussed in this book. The written signs that comprise what is confusingly called 'music' are merely a series of coded instructions to guide performers through the technicalities of producing the sounds we hear. Music does not exist on the printed page, and can only be fully appreciated and enjoyed as sound – a divine noise.

Listening skills – using your ears

The most important equipment necessary in the process of musical enjoyment is the human ear. You already have this equipment, but, like any other physical function, the process of listening can be developed and improved with practice. You can train your primary musical receiver (your ear) to enable you to pick up the music you hear more accurately. No special skills are required in order to achieve this aim, just some thought and concentration. In all modesty, I would suggest that the second piece of equipment you need would be this book, because it is necessary to have some knowledge of the way classical music is put together if you are to get the most out of it. We will go into this in more detail later in the book, but you will find that in a relatively short time you will become aware of all the various elements that make up a musical performance. There is so much more to listen for than the main themes of any given work. The famous tunes that are so familiar, and may have led you to want to know more about the music, do not appear in isolation. You will find that the composer has prepared the way for them and the musical narrative leading to the big tune is an interesting and exciting journey. Your enjoyment of the familiar part cannot fail to be heightened when you can appreciate the context in which it appears. We will explore the less obvious but equally rewarding parts of the pieces chosen as case studies by applying deep listening techniques, which I call 'listening below the surface'.

How to use this book

You have probably noticed that the volume in your hands is divided into two main sections, each taking up roughly half of the book. In the first part, we will examine the main types of musical forms that you are likely to encounter in the main repertoire of classical music. We will concentrate on the listening aspects, identifying themes, structures, melody, harmony and rhythm through a series of case studies. But do not worry, this

will all be done step-by-step. Technicalities will be kept to a minimum, and will not be allowed to get in the way of the music. Enjoyment is the key to learning here, and the one aim is to increase your listening pleasure.

In Part Two we will consider the historical context of the music, through a chronological approach from early music to the present day. Please do not think the two parts have to be worked through consecutively, as there is no reason why you should not move from one to the other. For example, if after you have worked through the Haydn case study in Chapter 01 you want to find out more about the composer, you could turn to the appropriate section in Part Two, read about his life and times, and discover how he fits into the larger picture of musical history. By the time you reach the end of the book, I hope you find your musical horizons have been extended, and that you are ready to proceed with confidence to whatever musical activity you please. There are some suggestions about further activities at the end of the book, but there is a huge world of classical music out there to be explored, and no two people will choose exactly the same route. Only one thing is certain – it is fun finding out. Let us begin our journey now by thinking about the very beginning of music, where it began, and how it works its magic upon us.

music – a common experience

We are all musical. We all respond to music, from early childhood to the end of our lives. Music is a means of communication as well as recreation. The process of enjoying a musical performance in the company of others provides a shared experience which is necessary for our social well-being and is common to all societies and cultures. Music is absolutely central to our existence. It is at the core of our being and one of the defining features of our humanity.

The ability of music to affect our moods and our health is increasingly being recognized through the growing practice of music therapy. Music is used to treat patients with various emotional and mental problems to the extent that music therapists are employed by many clinical establishments as a proven and effective part of the regime of treatment.

So why do we listen to music? Because it makes us feel good, or at least better. Whether it is used for therapeutic, commercial or recreation purposes, music can profoundly affect our feelings in many tangible ways. We don't know exactly how this happens, but we know from our own responses that it does, and that's enough to convince us of its value.

Now, the question arises, if this effect is the result of a natural and instinctive process, why do we need to learn about it? In particular, what's so special about classical music, that we should need a book to teach ourselves about it?

Most of us have experienced a moment when a particular combination of musical sounds produces a shiver of surprise, excitement and pleasure which is unique. This 'tingle factor' is highly addictive, and stimulates us to find out more about the phenomenon which produced the effect. The greater the knowledge and listening experience, the greater the pleasure and satisfaction. If it is classical music that provides your initial tingle, then you are entering a rich and exciting world of a music with a long and fascinating history, together with an accretion of formalities and conventions which you will get to grips with as you broaden your knowledge, understanding, and therefore enjoyment of the music.

What is classical music?

Nobody has yet come up with an adequate definition of 'classical music' as the term is understood today. It has been defined as 'serious' music, but this is seen now as deeply patronizing to other forms of music, such as jazz or folk, implying as it does that they are not to be taken seriously. For our purposes we need to take the broadest view possible, that is, music in the European tradition from medieval times to the present day. Other cultures have their own, equally important, classical musics, and these make fascinating study, but are generally beyond the scope of this book. The problem of defining classical music is further complicated by the fact that there is also a narrower view which is sometimes used by music historians and broadcasters. This takes the 'Classical period' to be roughly 1750 to 1830, typified by the music of Haydn and Mozart. We will look at this period and its music in Chapter 11, so don't worry if you come across the word 'classical' in this restricted sense.

In a concert hall you can expect to hear a range of music from about the last 250 to 300 years, which represents the repertoire of a typical symphony orchestra (we will look at the components of the orchestra as we go along). Most major cities have resident professional orchestras, which also perform in smaller towns within the area, so it is possible for many people to attend an orchestral concert without travelling too far. You may be thinking of confining yourself to building a collection of recorded music and/or listening to radio broadcasts, at least for the time being. This is fine, but, no matter how good your sound system is, there is nothing quite like the experience of hearing an orchestra 'in the flesh'.

Hearing and listening

Music is essentially a language, different from verbal communication, but it is not a foreign language. We have all been exposed to music from early childhood, so understanding classical music is simply a matter of expanding our innate aural vocabulary in the same way that we must expand our verbal vocabulary from childhood in order to appreciate works of literature. Like drama, music works on an emotional as well as an intellectual level; no one knows exactly how this happens, but it is undeniably real. Generally (but not always), the composer takes the listener on a musical journey in much the same way as the playwright constructs a plot, creating a series of contrasting tensions and relaxations, building a sense of anticipation which is finally resolved at the end of the piece. We will look at the different ways in which these effects are achieved, and how to recognize them, in Chapter 2.

Individual movements can be extracted from larger pieces and played separately, as is often the case on radio stations like UK's Classic FM, but, as we shall see, many composers develop their ideas over several thematically linked movements, which means that a work often makes more logical sense when listened to in its entirety. However, we shall begin our listening exercises by taking a single movement of a Haydn symphony, and putting it under the microscope to examine its component parts. The listening exercises are denoted by a symbol ▶ in the left-hand margin when they are on the CD. The works we shall be examining in these exercises are:

- Haydn, Symphony No. 94, 'Surprise', 2nd and 3rd movements

- Mozart, Symphony No. 40, 1st movement

- Mendelssohn, *Hebrides* overture, 'Fingal's Cave'

- Beethoven, Symphony No. 6, 'Pastoral'

- Debussy, *La Mer*

- Berlioz, *Symphony Fantastique*

- Wagner, 'Siegfried's Rhine Journey' from *Götterdämmerung*

- Stravinsky, *The Rite of Spring* (not on the CD)

- Mendelssohn, *A Midsummer Night's Dream* overture (not on the CD)

- Beethoven, Symphony No. 9, 'Choral' (discussed in Part Two, Chapter 12 – not on the CD)

There is a huge difference between merely hearing musical sounds and *listening* to the composer's ideas with knowledge and understanding. The first is purely a physical process by which we take in sounds for information, whereas the other involves a degree of conscious evaluation and focussing, similar to the process of understanding and translating spoken language into meanings and images. We are so accustomed to comprehending spoken language that we do it automatically, with no conscious effort, but we have forgotten that this is a skill which we acquired at a very early age. By concentrating on the language we heard around us, gradually understanding the spoken words and little by little extending our vocabulary, we were eventually able to understand all that was said. However, this is not a purely cognitive process, merely exposing children to language does not result in the child's acquisition of that language. There must be a meaningful interaction between the child and another person, usually a parent. So the all-important language skills are taught, with the parent as the child's first teacher.

Even though we first experienced music at about the same time that we encountered language, most of us were not encouraged to explore the music we heard in the same systematic way that our parents helped us to understand and speak the language which surrounded us. We *heard* music, but we were not all taught to *listen* to it. What we must do now is to begin to acquire and practise those skills which will help us to expand our musical horizons, and at the same time build up a store of background knowledge to extend the range of our musical experience.

Listening below the surface

▶ Case study 1 – Haydn, Symphony No. 94, 2nd movement

There are exercises we can do to sharpen up our aural perception, just like practising on a musical instrument to improve playing technique. What we are going to do to begin with is to listen to a well-known piece of music in a new and deeper way. The Haydn symphony movement described above, nicknamed the 'Surprise', is a good piece for this exercise because it is very simple and easy to remember.

In this first exercise we will think about the beginning of that simple tune, just the first 30 seconds or so, listening closely to the music and how it is played. We don't have to approach this music with too much reverence. The tune itself has no profound significance, in fact it sounds a bit like the nursery rhyme 'Twinkle, Twinkle, Little Star'. Pairs of short notes ascend and descend, slowly and quietly, followed by a pause (a sort of musical comma), after which the tune is repeated (even quieter this time), leading to the 'big bang' which gave the symphony its name. Haydn was not one to be po-faced about his music, as this tune shows. Musical jokes abound in his works and he intended his audiences to be entertained as they followed his musical story. The genius in this piece occurs not in the tune itself, but in what is done with it, in its **development**. This is a word which will crop up again later, and will be

discussed more fully in Chapter 03, when we return to the 'Surprise' to see where Haydn takes us.

Let's now try some more close listening. Play the tune again, and think about the following:

● Which instruments are playing the tune? Can you name them?

● Is the tune stated on its own, or is there any **accompaniment**?

● How is the tune played? In long or short notes, quick or slow, loud or soft?

● How has the composer used the instruments to create the final musical effect?

Summary of listening points

What have we heard in this very brief extract from Haydn's 'Surprise' Symphony?

● The instruments which comprise the string section of a symphony orchestra, and how they are divided into upper and lower strings.

Franz Joseph Haydn (1732–1809)

Stringed instruments

The orchestra is divided into four main sections: strings, woodwind, brass and percussion. The tune we are studying, Haydn's 'Surprise', is first played by the string section only, and the instruments involved are as follows, starting with the highest in pitch and working downwards: violins (usually divided into two sub-sections: first and second) and violas, described as the upper strings, plus 'cellos (short for violoncello) and double-basses (amazingly enough, the lower strings). All instruments in this family produce a sound by the vibration of the strings which are stretched across a hollow body and raised above it by means of a wedge placed beneath the strings, called a bridge. The body of the instrument serves to amplify the sound which the strings make when vibrating.

The two main species of stringed instruments are those which are plucked, like the harp and the guitar, and those which are sounded by the application of a bow of horsehair stretched across a hardwood stick. The bow is drawn across the strings to vibrate them and has the advantage of being capable of sustaining the note so produced. The instruments of the orchestral string family described above belong to this second category of bowed instruments. The violins and violas are held horizontally, supported under the player's chin, while the 'cello is played in a vertical position, the player sitting, supporting the instrument between the knees. The double-bass is also played in a vertical position, with the player either standing or sitting on a high stool. The bow is normally held in the right hand, and the strings are 'stopped' by the fingers of the left hand on the fingerboard, to alter the vibrating length of the string, and therefore the pitch of the note.

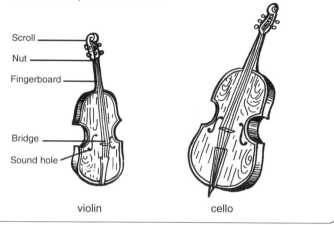

Scroll

Nut

Fingerboard

Bridge

Sound hole

violin   cello

- The difference between the tune and its accompaniment, and the groups of instruments that play each part.

- The way in which dynamics can be used to produce a dramatic effect.

More careful listening reveals that the tune itself is played by the violins only, slowly and very quietly. This is the superstructure, but what of the foundations? The tune is underpinned by the lower strings, which play a single longer note at the beginning of each phrase. Although not as easy to hear as the tune itself, this note plays an important part in filling out the sound, and without it the tune would sound much thinner and less effective. Despite the fact that the music is played at a very low volume, the tune and its accompaniment has the full weight of the orchestral string section.

So what's Haydn doing here? He is setting a scene for us – creating a mood which we can feel and share, as we follow his musical path. In presenting us with this simple tune and its accompaniment he is manipulating our emotional responses, and, once this control is established, he demonstrates his mastery by destroying the mood he has created. The quiet atmosphere is shattered by a massive orchestral hammer-blow. We suddenly see the purpose of the restricted instrumental palette which is used for the opening tune, and the extremely quiet presentation. The contrast could not be greater as every instrument joins in the blast at full volume. This is a clear, if not particularly subtle, example of the way a composer can use the orchestra to achieve a dramatic, emotional and humourous effect. The unexpected is always welcome in music of all kinds, and examples can be found in the work of the great composers throughout the history of music.

Degrees of loudness and softness in a musical com-position or performance are called **dynamics**, and Haydn was well aware of the effect that the dynamic contrasts in this symphony would have on at least some sections of his audience, as he is said to have remarked of his 'surprise' that 'the ladies will jump here!'. The nickname, like the names which have become attached to many other works, was not the composer's invention, but has been linked to the work through popular usage (the German nickname is *Paukenschlag* or 'drumstroke'). But more of Haydn and his music later when we return to this case study in Chapter 03.

elements of music

Melody

A melody is a varying series of pitches, which form a recognizable shape. This is a basic part of music, and one that is familiar to everyone. A very early example of melody occurred when monks began to chant the words of the Liturgy, varying the pitch of their voices to give greater effect. Many of these were said to have been catalogued and codified by Pope Gregory between 590 and 604, and continue to be used up to the present day. Gregorian chant, as it is called, using only the most basic elements of music, can produce a very beautiful and satisfying effect, and its continuing secular popularity bears witness to this. We also heard a very simple but effective melody in our Haydn example, played on the upper strings of the orchestra. But let's not be snobbish about the word – 'tune' will do just as well.

Harmony

Harmony occurs when two or more notes are sounded together. Notes are combined vertically to produce harmony as opposed to horizontally or serially in the case of melody. Western music has a highly developed system of harmonic organization and this is, as we might expect, exploited to the full by most composers. In the extract we studied in Chapter 01, the harmonic underpinning was initially provided by the lower strings, with their voices supporting the melody played by their colleagues 'upstairs'. When the full orchestra announced itself, the different instruments were playing notes which combined harmonically to form a **chord**, which is the name given to a group of notes sounded together. The juxtaposition of chords forms the basis of harmonic practice, and the way this is done will characterize a piece to a great extent. We will look at this in greater detail when we explore different musical styles.

Rhythm

All music has rhythm. Even the Gregorian chant mentioned above has a rhythm which is derived from the speech patterns of the Latin text, and in fact this is the most basic and natural form of rhythm. In our everyday speech we continually and unconsciously accent some syllables, lengthening, shortening and cutting them off to vary their sounds in order to make what we are saying intelligible and interesting to the listener, in other words, to communicate.

Musical communication is dependent upon the same type of variation of rhythms as speech. Note lengths and patterns are varied by rhythm, so it is the rhythmic element which characterizes the shape of the melodic message which is sent out to the listener. It is probable that the earliest form of music contained only rhythm, a stick beating against a hollow log perhaps, leading to the stretching of an animal skin over the log to form a primitive drum. Certainly, rhythm was a fundamental ingredient in the primeval soup of music and it has since been developed throughout the world, reaching the greatest degree of sophistication and complexity in the classical musics of Africa and India. In Western music, the strongest and most insistent rhythms are found in music which has its origins in dance. Conversely, a strongly rhythmic piece of music brings with it the desire to dance, or at least to tap our feet in time to the music. Haydn's music is almost always strongly rhythmic, and the 'Surprise' Symphony extract studied in Chapter 01 has a light but insistent 'walking' rhythm, which effectively sets the tone and the pace of the movement.

Time and pulse

The phrase 'in time to the music' implies a regular underlying beat or pulse, the speed of which sets the tempo (Italian for 'time'). If rhythm is the conversational shape of music, tempo is its very heartbeat. Like life itself, music exists in and moves with time. It's no coincidence that each section of a long piece is called a 'movement', confirming and reinforcing the impression of forward momentum.

The progress of a musical performance is measured by counting regular numbers of beats, in sets of predetermined length, constantly repeating. These little time capsules are known in the UK as 'bars' (Americans call them 'measures'). In written music, a line is drawn across the music at the end of every bar, hence the name. Bars provide a convenient method of measuring the length of a short piece or a section of a longer piece.

We will go on now to learn how to count bars – a useful skill – but, as the great conductor Sir Thomas Beecham

once advised his musicians, 'Remember that bars are only the boxes in which the music is packed.'

Feeling the pulse

Let's go back once more to our Haydn tune – you will know it pretty well by now. First, find the pulse of the music: the best way to do this is simply to relax and tap your foot along with the tune – each tap is one beat of the bar. The first beat of the bar is almost always slightly accentuated. With that walking rhythm you would expect to count in twos, and there are in fact two beats to the bar. Our melody begins on the first beat of the first bar, which simplifies matters greatly, but beware, it doesn't apply to every piece. Think, for example, of the opening of Beethoven's Fifth Symphony, those first three notes occur *before* the beginning of the first bar. So, counting two beats in each bar, we find our Haydn melody lasts for eight bars. This is repeated, and the big orchestral chord occurs in the sixteenth bar. We will be returning to this piece in Chapter 03, when we consider how composers develop their musical material.

Once you know how to find the pulse, and identify the first beat of the bar, you can practise this skill by listening to different pieces, and applying what you have learnt. The character of the music can help here, for example a waltz always has three beats to a bar, and a march two. Of course you already knew that, but maybe hadn't thought about it. Think about it now and apply it to a new piece of your choice; it may fit. If not, think again. When you are sure of the number of beats in the bar, you are ready to count the number of bars taken up by the new melody that you can identify.

Most programme notes for concerts, and books on music, assume this ability and casually refer to, say, a 16-bar theme, expecting the reader to be able to follow this description and identify the theme. Once you can do this, you have improved your understanding of music. You are better equipped to recognize and describe the structure of an unfamiliar piece of music and to follow the composer's scheme of ideas. It's not difficult, and you will have in your possession one of the essential tools you need in order to further your knowledge, and hence your enjoyment, of music.

the musical journey

When we first begin to enjoy classical music, one of the factors to contend with is the sheer length of some of the pieces. The longer works can seem daunting to the newcomer, for example, a symphony by Bruckner can take well over an hour to play. But we don't need to dive into the deep end right away; there are many hundreds of excellent works that take only a few minutes to make their musical point.

The factors which influence the length of a piece of music are diverse, but they could involve the conventions of the period, nature and style of the piece, and, all too often, the desires and specifications of an employer or patron. Generally though, the duration of a musical work is artistically determined by the composer's skill and inspiration in the extent to which the musical ideas are developed. There are numerous frameworks which could be employed, and in this chapter we will look at the most commonly used forms and learn how to recognize them.

Symphony and overture

The names given to compositions don't necessarily give an indication of their duration or style. The **symphony**, for example, is probably the best-known type of classical piece, but it varies massively according to the identity and historical period of the composer. You could be forgiven for assuming that some orchestras played little or nothing else but symphonies. In fact, their names suggest as much, like the London, Chicago and City of Birmingham Symphony orchestras, to pick out three from the many to be found throughout the world. Of course, the symphony is only one of the musical forms played by these orchestras, but it has been the vehicle for some of the most profound and memorable musical statements from the middle of the eighteenth century onwards.

Before that time, the word 'symphony' was used indiscriminately to describe a piece of instrumental music, usually for a group of instruments, but occasionally even for a solo work. It is not unusual, for example, to see a short instrumental introduction to a seventeenth- or early eighteenth-century opera described as 'sinfonia'. Nowadays, the conventional description of such a piece would be **overture**, but at that time the two terms were practically synonymous. Regularized forms of overtures did gradually emerge, however. The two main variations of the species were French and Italian, both of which were split into three sections. The Italian version was fast–slow–fast, while the French overture was made up of a slow introduction, followed by a quick section and concluded with a stately dance, usually a **minuet**.

Many early symphonies were structured on one or other of these models. The English composer William Boyce (1711–79) produced no less than 20 symphonies, all based on the Italian or French overture. They were actually first performed as overtures and interludes in his larger theatrical works, but, in 1760 he collected together eight pieces he thought suitable for concert performance and published them as 'symphonys'. They are delightful miniatures, some lasting only a few minutes (all eight take up just one hour and fit conveniently on to a CD), packed with lively, memorable tunes. If you haven't come across them before, they are well worth a listen.

Wind Instruments

Boyce used the basic orchestra of his time. A body of strings as described in Chapter 01, comprising violins, violas, cellos and double basses, plus wind instruments of the two main types, woodwind and brass.

Woodwind

All wind instruments produce a sound by the vibration of a column of air within an enclosed tube. In some woodwind instruments, a cane reed is vibrated by the pressure of the player's breath, thereby agitating the air stream. Boyce's orchestra makes particular use of oboes (the composer describes them as 'hoyboys', a corruption of the French *haut bois* or 'high wood', which eventually became anglicized as 'oboe'), with their incisive tone produced by the double reed which is placed between the player's lips.

The flute is the one woodwind instrument which does not have a reed, but is sounded by the player blowing across a tube, bored with finger holes (nowadays covered with keys), to alter the pitch. Originally made of wood, the modern instrument is more likely to be metal. Boyce specified the German flute, which was also known as the transverse flute, to distinguish it from the end-blown flute or recorder, which was often seen in orchestras up to the mid eighteenth century. The bassoon, a large double-reed instrument, played verically, with a narrow tube connecting the reed to the body of the instrument, was the third member of the woodwind section. It was often used to reinforce or 'double' the line played by the basses. The clarinet was not yet part of the orchestra, so we will look at it later.

Brass

Some of the symphonies call for horns and trumpets. These would have been natural instruments (see illustration below), with none of the valves and extra tubing that we see on modern instruments. The sound is produced by the player's lips vibrating within a small, cup-like mouthpiece, the pitch of the notes being altered by tightening or relaxing the lip muscles to produce respectively higher or lower notes. Both of these instruments have outdoor origins. The horn was to be found in the hunting field, and the trumpet was the province of the military. They have often been used to evoke their origins, with the horn providing a pastoral lilt and the trumpet signifying ceremony or conflict. These are stereotypes to listen for, but they also have other voices and characters which can be quite surprising. Boyce uses them conventionally, but to great effect in the fifth symphony. We will look at the other members of the brass family later.

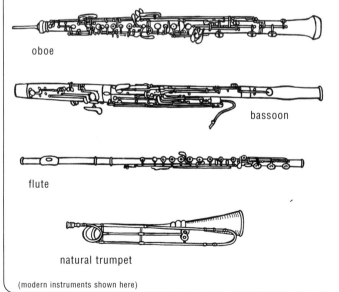

oboe

bassoon

flute

natural trumpet

(modern instruments shown here)

natural horn

If we put together the characteristics of the Italian and French overtures, we can construct a work with four separate sections: fast, slow, minuet, fast. This is broadly the pattern of the symphony which emerged during the eighteenth century and formed the framework for many of the greatest orchestral compositions for the next 200 years. Each section is expanded and is now called a **movement**. In works for small groups or single instruments (**chamber music**), a similar four-movement structure is found in the **sonata**. In fact, you could say that a symphony is an orchestrated sonata. Similarly, a work with a title like trio, quartet or quintet can be expected to conform to the same four-movement pattern, always remembering that this applies to the period from about 1750 onwards (earlier forms of the sonata are discussed in Chapter 09).

It is difficult to lay down hard-and-fast rules about musical forms, because composers are creative artists and the essence of creativity is change. New methods and combinations of sounds are constantly being invented, and it is the duty of an artist to challenge the assumptions and conventions of the day. This means that we can never take a rigid view of compositional form, or expect a work to conform to a scientifically accurate pattern. The genius of the composer often lies in producing the unexpected, deviating from the well-beaten path which would lead to boredom. We'll be looking at examples of symphonies by different composers as we go on, but it is important to have a basic idea of the form to begin with. If you know the rules, you can better appreciate the composer's point in breaking them.

The concerto

Briefly, a work for a solo instrument or a group of instruments, with orchestral accompaniment can be given the title **concerto**. As with the symphony, the meaning changes according to historical period. In early music the term could be used indiscriminately to describe a work for voices accompanied by a group of instruments, or even an unaccompanied solo piece. By the time of Bach and Handel (the first half of the eighteenth century), the form became refined into the **concerto grosso**, in which a group of solo instruments, the **concertino**, were balanced by the accompanying orchestral body, the **ripieno**. A three-movement structure was the norm, normally following the fast–slow–fast pattern of the Italian overture. Bach's set of six

Brandenburg Concertos (1721) contain excellent examples of this type of work and are discussed in greater detail in Chapter 10.

The solo concerto, like the symphony, became formalized in the mid eighteenth century. The three-movement form was retained, but a single solo instrument was pitted against the full force of the orchestra, making for a greater contrast between soloist and accompaniment. As always, there are exceptions to the rule, and concertos for two or three solo instruments crop up from time to time. These are called double or triple concertos, according to the number of soloists. Beethoven's Triple Concerto for violin, piano and cello is a supreme example of this kind of work, calling for an exceptional degree of sensitivity from its executants to maintain a balance between the solo instruments and the orchestral forces. Beethoven presents us with a chamber group (a piano trio) on the platform with a full orchestra. But many artists have proved that it is quite possible to transcend the problem of balance, and emphasize instead the unique musical qualities of the work.

There are many more factors of historical interest and performance practice to be considered. We will look at these in the following chapters, but for the moment we are considering the broad frameworks in which composers present their ideas. Remember that the terminology differs for orchestral and chamber music. A performance for one or two instruments is described as a **recital**, while the word **concert** is used when larger forces are employed.

The musical material

We have found out something of the basic structure of many of the best-known orchestral and chamber works, how many movements to expect, and of their relative character. We now need to move in a little closer and see some of the ways in which the composer organizes the musical ideas within these larger frameworks. Generally, a movement within a larger piece like a symphony will contain only one or two melodic themes. This is the raw material which the composer will work on and develop during the course of the movement. There are various ways in which this material can be altered and reworked to form a logical, coherent and persuasive musical argument which will deliver an emotionally satisfying experience. This is the ultimate payoff: the reward for following the composer's musical thought processes, and experiencing the drama, excitement, pathos, calm and ultimate resolution as the story unfolds.

The potential development of a musical theme is limited only by the composer's imagination and ingenuity. The basic elements of music (as set out in Chapter 02), are all available, plus the instruments of the orchestra. Here is some of the ammunition in the musical arsenal:

- The orchestral palette is enormous, and thousands of permutations of instrumental colour are possible. A melody can be transformed by switching from one instrument to another. This is the art of **orchestration**.

- The dynamic range can be manipulated to great effect, as we experienced in our Haydn example in Chapter 01.

- The tempo can be speeded up or slowed down.

- The rhythmic patterns can be changed, altering the character of a melodic line.

- It is possible to change the mood of a melody harmonically, by substituting different chords in the accompaniment.

- Finally, the melody itself can be transformed in various ways.

Key

Tension and relaxation can be created by changing **key**, a difficult concept to explain in words. Basically, if a melody is transposed so that it begins on a different note from the original pitch, it is said to have changed key. For our present purposes, we can assume that any piece of music has a 'home' key, in which it starts and finishes. So when we see a piece described as being in the key of, say, G major (as is the 'Surprise' Symphony), we know that G is the 'home' key, in which the music begins and ends. During a movement, we can expect to travel to different keys, some quite near, others more remote, before returning home.

Major and minor

It is also common for composers to change between major and minor versions of the same key. This means that the 'home' key is based upon the same note, but a different kind of chord is built upon it. The difference between major and minor is very distinctive. Most listeners would say that the major is bright, and the minor darker, or even use adjectives like 'happy' and 'sad' to describe major and minor, but it is dangerous to apply such stereotypes to music, as happy tunes have been written in minor keys, and vice versa. Such judgements are always subjective, and you will have the chance to make up your own mind when we listen to more of the 'Surprise' symphony later in this chapter.

We don't need to delve very deeply into the technicalities, but you will get used to the sound and feeling of music which is changing key or **modulating**, as this is a commonly used tool in the composer's kit. Don't worry – you already know what this sounds like, it's just a matter of recognizing these changes when they happen, and thereby understanding what the composer is doing. We have enough facts for the moment. It's time to listen to some more music.

Charting the journey

▶ Case study 1 *continued*

Let's return to the second movement of Haydn's 'Surprise' Symphony. As we noted above, the work is described as being in the key of G major, but this movement takes as its home base the key of C major, closely related to G, which is the key for all the other movements. The structure of the symphony is typical of its period (1792), comprising four movements: fast (with a short, slow introduction), slow, minuet, fast. The second movement is described as **andante** (it was the convention to put tempo instructions in Italian, whatever the nationality of the composer, and the Austrian Haydn observes this), meaning literally 'moving along', not quite slow, but slowish. That walking, two-in-a-bar rhythm we observed in Chapter 01 is a typical andante.

The theme

In Chapter 01, we restricted our listening to the first 16 bars: up to the 'big bang'. If we let the music run on, we discover that we have listened to only half of the tune. The second half is similar in character to the first, but there are a number of differences. The melody is not quite the same, and it is more ornate, all the strings have more notes to play, and flute, oboe and horns join in to thicken the orchestral texture. The rhythmic patterns do not alter, giving a feeling of continuity. Like the first half of the tune, the conclusion is made up of an eight-bar section, which is repeated. So the musical subject matter, or **theme**, of this movement is 32 bars long, divided into two equal halves, which are themselves split into two repeated eight-bar statements.

Perhaps you can hear that the 'surprise' chord, halfway through the theme, is not based on the notes you heard in the opening bar. Haydn has taken us into a different key (actually G, the nearest relative of C) with the surprise, but this is not maintained; the second half of the theme remains firmly in the home or **tonic** key. What we have in this theme is a good example of **binary form**, a simple piece divided into two sections, both repeated. Early dance music was often constructed along these lines, and seventeenth-century composers employed the form for instrumental pieces. Haydn has taken a well-used and easily recognizable pattern for the theme of this movement, all the better to provide the basis for embellishment. The simple theme is a canvas on which the composer weaves a beautiful tapestry of sounds. The movement consists of the theme, plus a series of four exquisite variations, each of which develops and transmutes the commonplace melody to something more precious. Listen again to the theme, noting the different sections and repeats as described above, then consider the first variation. What happens here?

First variation

The parts that were played by the first and second violins in the first statement of the theme have been moved down, so that they now appear, unchanged, in the second violins and violas respectively. The first violins are now free to play an astoundingly beautiful counter-melody or **descant** above the theme. Haydn puts a thread of gold into the commonplace fabric of the basic material. This delicate filigree is worked mainly by the strings, with a flute providing a little reinforcement towards the end of the first section. The variation is presented quietly, with great poise and delicacy.

Second variation

Listen particularly for the change in character in the next variation, because here we enter the world of the minor key. Haydn helps us by announcing the changed theme loudly in strings and woodwind. Part two of the melody is decorated by rippling scale passages by both woodwind and strings with trumpets and timpani (see 'Percussion' below) added towards the end to reinforce the orchestral texture. Did you notice the different atmosphere created by the minor? How would you describe it?

I think it sounds slightly menacing and unsettling, those fast string and woodwind passages towards the end give a feeling of restlessness. At the end of this variation we get a little quiet passage played on the first violins only (four bars long if you're counting), which leads us gently back to our original major, and forms a transition from 'dark' to 'light'. That's only one view of this variation and you may hear it differently, which is fine – one of the great things about music is that there is no single 'correct' way of listening to a piece.

Third variation

The major key is restored for this variation. Now the melody is stated by the oboes, repeating each note four times instead of two, for the first eight bars, with strings providing the accompaniment. After this the tune returns to the strings, with the woodwind playing some quite new counter-melodies. The mood of this variation is fairly subdued, and the dynamic level low. After its completion, there is a moment of contemplation before the full force of the orchestra is once more unleashed.

Fourth variation

Here we have a dynamic contrast of almost similar proportions to that which gives the symphony its name. All of the instruments are called upon to announce the first eight bars of the theme, but the melody is given to the brass and woodwind, with the lower strings and timpani giving a rhythmic and harmonic underpinning. The first violins, in the meantime, maintain a rippling counter-melody that adds a thrilling extra element to the excitement of the full orchestra. This is alternated with a passage of similar length for strings and bassoon, before the orchestra returns to complete the theme. The end of the movement approaches, but Haydn adds a tailpiece, or, more formally, a **coda** where, for a moment the direction of the music is uncertain, there is a suggestion of a key change, but finally this resolves into a last, peaceful, brief statement of the opening tune. This enchanting movement takes its leave as quietly as it entered, with elegance and dignity.

We have looked at one short movement of one of Haydn's symphonies (he wrote 104) in great detail, and

Percussion (1)

It is probable that the earliest musical instruments were struck or shaken to produce their sounds. The modern orchestra has a whole battery of such instruments, albeit much more sophisticated than their early ancestors. You may have seen them arrayed at the back of the platform at a concert, sometimes referred to by musicians as the 'kitchen sink department'. They fall into two main categories, tuned and untuned, which means that some can produce an identifiable note or set of notes when struck, whereas others make a sound of indefinite pitch. The timpani, or kettle drums belong in the first category. They look like large copper-coloured pots, or inverted domes, with a thin membrane (originally calfskin, but now a type of plastic) stretched across the open end. These are tuned to the pitch of the key-note of the work to be played, and to the nearest related notes. Other drums, like the bass drum (large) and the side drum (small), have no definite pitch, though they produce a very distinctive sound. We will meet more members of the percussion family (tuned and untuned) later.

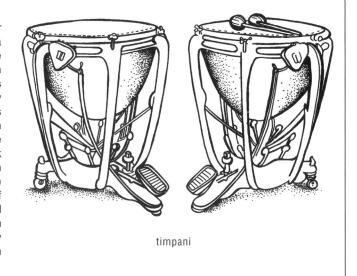

timpani

I hope you agree that there is a huge amount of interesting music to listen to, even in such a short, unassuming piece. Often the lower, or accompanying parts prove to contain the most moving material, and a master composer like Haydn would use all of the resources at his disposal to keep the full attention of his audience. At that time (1792), a fairly sophisticated audience such as Haydn's would have been well aware of the formal conventions of the music, and would have definite ideas of what to expect from a symphony, the number of movements, their character and length. The music beguiles by a clever juxtaposition of the expected and the unexpected; providing the comfort of a well-known format, plus the excitement of the musical surprises that the composer builds into the formal framework. So the little twists and turns, and contrasts of mood, key and dynamics that we have been examining would have been appreciated to the full by the original audience. By understanding these conventions and devices, we can enjoy the music, despite the very different types of music and culture that we have experienced in our lives.

inside the symphony

In this chapter you will learn:

- about the third movement of the Surprise Symphony and the origins of sonata, or first movement form

- about our second case study: the first movement of Mozart's Symphony No. 40

- about a new instrument – the clarinet.

The minuet and the scherzo

We noticed that the tune Haydn used as a basis for the variations is in a simple binary form (A–B). The next logical step from there would be to create a **ternary** structure, with three sections, A–B–A. The third movement of the 'Surprise' Symphony, the Minuet, is in fact patterned on this ternary model. The minuet was originally a French dance, of moderate speed and in triple time (that is, with three beats to the bar), which, before the pivotal date c.1750, often formed part of a **suite** of dances. This was a form which reached the heights of expression in the hands of J. S. Bach, and to which we shall return later, in Part Two. The minuet as a movement within the symphony was a remnant of the dance suite. As noted above, the movement has a three-part structure, which comprises the first minuet (A), followed by a second contrasting minuet (B), sometimes called a trio (because the original practice was to score this section for three instruments), after which there is a return to the beginning and a repetition of the first minuet (A). In our Haydn example, the first minuet is for full orchestra, while the second minuet (marked 'trio' on the **score**) is played by the strings, with a single bassoon doubling the first violin line. Each minuet is in two sections, and all sections are repeated. It would be a good idea now to stop reading and spend five minutes listening to this movement (track 2 on your CD). Can you identify the different sections? Play the track again if you are not sure. Listen below the surface for the deep, reedy sound of the bassoon in the middle section.

▶ Haydn, Symphony No. 94, 3rd movement

The character of the minuet, as a symphonic movement, often returned to its rustic roots, this tendency marking a progression away from the formal strictures of the dance suite towards a freer vehicle for the composer's ideas. It was the mighty hand of Beethoven (1770–1828), that brought about the demise of the minuet, when he substituted a **scherzo** (literally 'joke') in most of his later symphonies. Incidentally, Haydn had used the term 'scherzo and trio' in his six string quartets, Op. 33 (Op. is short for **Opus**, which means simply 'work'), but the movements so described were minuets in all but name. The Beethovenian scherzo is usually fast and vivacious, its boisterous character providing a contrast with the composer's portentous and sometimes sombre slow movements. Many later composers included scherzos in their symphonies. In fact, after Beethoven, the minuet ceased to be a part of the scheme of the symphony or the sonata.

Sonata form

First impressions are important and, not unnaturally, most composers design the first movement of their works to make the maximum impact. Consequently, a more elaborate structure was devised for the opening movement of major pieces like symphonies, sonatas, concertos and quartets. A word should be said here about the overture, out of which the symphony developed, as we have seen, and which itself meta-morphosed into a single-movement work, no longer having to prelude any form of dramatic or operatic per-formance. The concert overture became a free-standing piece, which generally had the same basic structure as the first movement of the longer works mentioned above.

A durable form was necessary to sustain all of these types of composition, and to survive, as it has, for more than 200 years. The structure had to be recognizable, yet flexible, in order to give the listener some familiar frame of reference, and, at the same time, allow the composer the freedom to introduce new ideas. This first-movement form, or **sonata form** is based upon the ternary idea, but modifying it allows the composer more room for creative expression. The basic form, then, is simple, but the possibilities of complication are endless. Let's look at the foundations first, then see what can be built upon them.

The three-part design (A–B–A) governs the structure of the movement, but the difference between this and the previous idea of the ternary is that the middle (B) section contains not new material, but a modification or reworking of the musical ideas that have already been presented. The three sections are now described as the exposition (A), followed by the development (B) and the recapitulation (A). To complicate matters, the exposition is normally (but not always) divided into two, with sep-arate themes (or groups of themes), the first and second subject, and the whole movement is topped off with a coda; an idea we have already encountered in our examination of the Haydn 'Surprise' movement, in Chapter 03.

The **development** section is sometimes called the **free fantasia,** and indeed the composer does have the freedom to take the subject matter in any direction, making use of any or all of the musical devices listed in Chapter 03. A prominent feature of this section is the tendency of composers to display their virtuosity by means of adventures in **tonal** movement. Thus the thematic material is taken through several different keys, some quite remote from the 'home' key, in which the music begins. The effect of this on the listener is unsettling, though pleasurably so. A dramatic tension is created by the uncertainty of a shifting tonality. The ground literally moves beneath our feet as we are taken on a journey into unfamiliar territory. Of course we know we will eventually be returned safely to our home base, but, in the hands of a skilful composer, a sonata-form movement can be an exhilarating roller-coaster ride.

One of the most attractive features of sonata form, which may go some way to explaining its enduring popularity with composers, is that it can be changed and adapted by new generations of composers while still retaining its general character. It would be a mistake to lay down strict rules for sonata form, as exceptions could always be found. First and second subject groups can contain several themes, and new material can be introduced in the development section. Furthermore, modified versions of sonata form can be found in movements other than the opening one, most commonly in the **finale,** or last movement.

Enjoying the journey

Because sonata form provides the building blocks for many of the major works of the best-known composers, it's worth spending a little time getting familiar with it. You have probably heard some pieces which are constructed on the sonata principle, but now you can listen to them in a more thoughtful way, applying some of the listening techniques we have acquired so far. First let's choose a piece, a suitable subject for our investi-gation. I would recommend Haydn or Mozart to begin with, because their works are more concisely expressed than many later composers, and they conform more precisely to the principles set out above, although we can always expect a few surprises!

So, how about a little Mozart? The first movement of the Symphony No. 40 (his second to last, completed in 1788), is a good example of sonata form in action, and a showcase for Mozart's mature genius. It is also good for us to listen to because the themes are simple, memorable and well contrasted. The movement goes straight into the first subject without any form of introduction. What we must do as our principal task is identify and remember the main themes, or subjects, of this movement so that we can follow their development and recognize them when they return.

Words about music

We should pause here for a minute, and consider the problems inherent in talking, and writing, about music. A tune cannot be translated exactly into words. We have already drawn an analogy between music and language (Chapter 01), but the two remain separate and different forms of communication. We can observe certain things about a tune, such as whether the melody rises or falls, uses long or short notes, is loud or soft, and so on, as we have already done, but this does not *identify* the music. These characteristics may well be true as far as they go, but they do not give you enough information to go away whistling the tune. That can be acquired only by listening.

We can go further and describe the mood of a piece, using words which describe the human emotions generated by the music like 'happy', 'sad', 'angry' and so forth. This is essentially subjective, of course, as a piece may arouse different emotions in different people. But if you are looking for a shorthand way of identifying a theme, so that you can pick it out when it reappears, you could do worse than trust your emotional responses. For example, one eighteenth-century critic, after hearing a performance of our first case study, wrote: 'The surprise might not be unaptly likened to the situation of a beautiful shepherdess who, lulled to slumber by the murmur of a distant waterfall, starts alarmed by the unexpected firing of a fowling piece.' Is that the picture the music conveys to you? No, nor me, but perfectly valid all the same.

What this is leading up to is that we are now going to find words to describe and differentiate the two major musical subjects that form the basis of the first movement of our Mozart symphony. So, being fully aware of the approximate nature of verbal description, we can proceed with caution. Please listen now to the beginning of the symphony, keeping in mind the overall structure which governs the movement: the sonata principle.

Exposition, development, recapitulation

▶ Case study 2 – Mozart, Symphony No. 40, 1st movement
Exposition – first subject
This is quite brief, in this case just over seven minutes but some conductors set a faster tempo than others (we will look at performance practice in more detail in Chapter 08). While you listen, try asking yourself a few questions which might help you to fix the characteristics of the music in your mind. Here are a few examples:

1 Can you hear a definite tune?

2 Is it fast or slow, loud or soft?

3 Does the melody rise or fall, that is, do the notes go up or down?

4 Think about the distance between the notes in the melody; are they large or small? Are there any big jumps in the tune or does it seem to proceed smoothly in consecutive steps?

5 What about the rhythm? Does the tune have a distinctive rhythm which is repeated, like a drum beat, or is it smooth and flowing, without any disturbances?

6 Which instruments are playing the tune? (You could confine this answer to groups of instruments, like upper or lower strings, woodwind, brass and/or percussion).

7 Finally, you could let your imagination run free and choose a word to describe the tune in emotional terms, such as 'tearful', 'cheeky', 'funereal', 'bouncy', or however the melody strikes you. This is a personal exercise. Different people will come up with different adjectives, but you are making your own label to identify this tune for yourself, so it doesn't matter which word you choose, as long as it means something to you.

Let's listen again to the opening of the movement thinking about the questions above.

1 I think you will agree that there is a definite tune. It is short (about 30 seconds long), and is rather abruptly

pushed aside by a secondary theme which provides a period of transition, a changing of gears, before the second subject is announced.

2 It's quite fast, marked **allegro molto** (it was conventional in Mozart's time to write tempo directions in Italian) which means 'very quick'. If you want to, you can count two beats to the bar – the tune begins at the end of the first bar, and the transitional passage appears at bar 28. The music begins quietly, and remains so until the loud chord breaks into it at the start of the transition, the sudden dynamic change altering the mood. We are familiar with this device now, having encountered it in our Haydn movement, in Chapter 01.

3/4 The little melodic figure, made up of three notes, which is heard at the beginning, is the germ out of which much of the musical material in this movement grows. It is made up of a single downward step, with the lower note then repeated. This three-note figure is itself repeated, twice, followed by an upward leap. The first subject is characterized by this simple musical phrase, out of which grows the opening theme. The music descends step by step from the high peak attained by the leap, and this process is repeated at a pitch reduced by one note. The contrast between sudden ascents and smooth stepwise movement created a satisfying melodic balance which was particularly important to Mozart's audience.

5 That first three-note figure, taken rhythmically, is even more prolific. Two short notes, followed by one long (in Morse code it would be dot–dot–dash), appear in all the instrumental parts during those first 27 bars of music, and can be found woven deeply into the fabric of the entire movement. When that rhythmic pattern is repeated on one note, it does in fact sound a little drum-like and is used as an underpinning for more languid chords in the wind section the second half of the first subject (bars 16–19).

6 The melody is first heard in the upper strings (first and second violins to be precise), with violas, cellos and double-basses providing the accompaniment. The woodwind (flutes, clarinets and bassoons) join in at bar 14.

7 This is your chance to think of a word or words to describe the first subject tune. I would choose words like 'jaunty', 'jolly' or 'bouncy' – it certainly jogs along at a good, breezy pace – but it's really up to you. If you want to call it, 'tune no. 1', that's all right, as long as you can recall all the details of it. Let's just pause for a minute and look at the information we've collected about the tune.

Summary of first subject

It's a distinctive, fast tune, played quietly on strings at first, with woodwind joining in later. The three-note figure, or **motif** recurs in all parts, and is probably going to play an important part in the movement, both melodically and rhythmically.

We now have our aural information about the first subject, and are fully prepared to follow it in its progress through the movement. We have looked at this first brief section of the symphony in great detail, in order to formulate a checklist for listening in depth, and not to miss any vital musical clues we may need to remember as the movement develops. Now it should be easier to apply the same criteria to the second subject. First we must identify it.

Exposition – second subject

Luckily, there is a good, clear indicator to mark the beginning of the second subject. After the bridge passage, or transition mentioned earlier, the loud 'gear changing', there is one bar of complete silence. The second subject then begins, quietly, in the strings. Listen to the recording now and see if you can spot the silent bar (if you're still counting, it's bar 43).

Of course you can find it, because Mozart wanted you to. To help you, he put a musical 'full stop' in the previous bar. Thinking of all the points we applied to the first subject, we should be able to summarize the second subject in the same way. Listen to the new material several times, and think about its characteristics (it might help to write them down). It's not very long, only a matter of 22 bars (44–66).

Summary of second subject

As mentioned above, the quiet tune begins in the strings, but, unlike the first subject, it is shared by the woodwind, as clarinet and bassoon take over very quickly, after which there is a dialogue between the strings and woodwind, with one section following on from the other in succession, taking it in turns to play different parts of the melody. This does not sound disjointed, as you might

The clarinet

Mozart gets the credit for being the first composer to explore the potential of this remarkable instrument. As well as intro-ducing it into his orchestral scores, he wrote a clarinet concerto and quintet (for clarinet plus string quartet). The clarinet is a woodwind instrument, the sound being produced by means of a single, blade-like, cane reed, which is fastened to a hollow mouthpiece and held between the player's lips. The instrument has three distinct registers, each with its characteristic sound. By increasing lip pressure, or 'overblowing' as it is called, a note is produced which is 12 notes higher than the original. The low register (sometimes called *chalumeau*, after a more basic precursor of the clarinet) has a full, dark sound. The middle range of the instrument produces a smooth, liquid 'milk chocolate' sound (these are my adjectives, beware of their subjective nature as discussed earlier), while the upper register is brighter, even piercing. and capable of great dramatic intensity in an orchestral context. In the hands of a good player, the clarinet is capable of executing extremely brilliant **virtuoso** passages, moving nimbly between registers to great effect as a solo instrument. Finally, the clarinet also has a distinguished place in the history of jazz, and players such as Benny Goodman have made outstanding contributions in both the classical and jazz fields.

Types of clarinet

The instrument comes in various sizes, including a bass clarinet, which has a metal bell-section at the bottom and a curved tube at the top, making it look a little like a saxophone (see page 91). There is also a basset clarinet, which also has a small bell, and is sometimes used in Mozart's clarinet concerto to provide an extended lower register, which some players insist the composer intended. This should not be confused with the basset horn, which is pitched lower and looks like a small bass clarinet. Mozart wrote specifically for this instrument in his opera *The Magic Flute*, as did Richard Strauss in *Elektra*.

clarinet

bass clarinet

expect, because the parts are knitted together so well in the orchestration. The tempo is the same as for the first subject, but the main tune is more 'polished' (again, this is my adjective – you may want to use a different word) in character with a smooth downward progression of notes which appears in the clarinets and violins. Towards the end of this short section, there is a gradual increase in volume, a **crescendo**, which leads into the closing part of the exposition (or **codetta**). Here the three-note motif returns, spread throughout the orchestra, and gradually the orchestral texture thickens, that is to say that more instruments are employed, and in the closing bars the motif is repeated until a final full-stop (or cadence, as it is properly called) announces that the exposition section of the movement is completed.

At this point, Mozart writes an instruction to return to the beginning, and repeat the whole of the exposition. According to the discretion of the conductor, exposition repeats are not always observed in performance, but in our recording, we do hear the section twice. We have now arrived at bar 100 (Mozart was very precise in the architecture of this movement, as many scholars have pointed out), and, assuming the exposition is not repeated, please listen to the end of the movement, and see if you can identify the development and recapitulation.

Development

Remember that there are no hard and fast rules in the development section. A composer may refer to any of the material in the exposition in any order, or may use fragments of the subject matter, or even introduce new themes. In this case, Mozart chooses to concentrate on the first subject material for his development. But what has happened to the tune? It is perfectly recognizable, but has changed. It has been destabilised because the familiar key base has been removed. Instead the melody shifts restlessly from key to key. The comfortable rug has been pulled from beneath our feet, and we are being taken away from our familiar 'home' surroundings. But, it's exciting to go on an excursion away from the predictable into the unknown. How can we keep up with Mozart as he takes off to unfamiliar territory?

This is where the simple rhythmic nature of the theme proves useful. It gives us a signpost with which we can map our journey. We can rely on it to carry us through the development section of this movement. The three-note motif is all-pervading, and runs through the music like a thread, binding the material together. As the development progresses and the tune becomes more remote from the 'home' key, the volume of the music is increased and the orchestral texture thickens (all the instruments are busy). This marks the climactic point in the movement, the development is at its height. Gradually, the texture thins and the mood becomes more subdued and quieter, in preparation for the return of the first subject in its original form.

Recapitulation

There is a feeling of relaxation when the 'home' key is restored, but do not expect a carbon copy of the exposition. Mozart decides to extend the transition passage between first and second subjects, and presents us with what amounts almost to mini-development. We wonder where this will lead us, until the silent bar signals a return to the second subject and finally to the coda, which makes much play of the now familiar triple-note figure, which the orchestra triumphantly proclaims to close the movement.

I hope you were able to follow the musical journey through this sonata form movement without too much difficulty. A good understanding of this type of structure will give you the listening equipment you need to tackle longer pieces which might seem daunting at first. The thing to do next is practise this skill by listening to as many examples as you can, until you are confident about your ability to recognize the form. As we noted earlier, the first movement of symphonies, sonatas, quartets, quintets, trios, concertos, plus concert overtures written between about 1750 and 1900, would be fairly safe places to expect to encounter the sonata principle.

You could practise on the rest of the 'Surprise' Symphony (not on the CD) if you wish, the first and fourth movements are both in sonata form, but watch out – the first movement begins with a slow introduction, which is not part of the scheme. None of this introductory material is developed or repeated. The sonata pattern begins at bar 18, when the tempo changes from a slow triple to a quick duple (2 beats to the bar) as the first subject proper begins.

The symphony is a good example of its kind, and when you have studied the two outer movements it would be a good idea to run through the whole work, to take in the larger view of the scheme of this classical symphony. Notice the way the different characters of the movements follow and complement each other to produce a well-balanced and satisfying musical experience.

painting pictures in sound

05

In this chapter you will learn:

● about three very different works: Mendelssohn's overture *Hebrides,* Beethoven's sixth symphony (*Pastoral*) and Debussy's *La Mer.*

Until now in our discussion of classical music, we have thought about music as a self-contained language, which, though governed by rules, forms and conventions, speaks to us directly, without reference to anything outside itself. We noted the difference between words and music as methods of communication, how words come equipped with the baggage of pre-conceived meanings and images which may differ in individuals, but nevertheless offer a definite image. In the case of music, the question arises of whether it is capable of representing anything other than its own repertoire of sounds. But many composers have been inspired by extra-musical matters, such as places, people and folk tales. Of course, music cannot describe a specific object like, say, a boat, but it can convey an idea of the movement of the sea, and the imagination then conjures up the nautical images to complete the picture. Music creates the emotional conditions to stimulate the imagination.

Evoking non-musical images

How can a composer, through a purely musical idiom, create a world outside the purely abstract, given only the colours of the musical palette? The first, and most obvious, way is direct imitation of extra-musical sounds. For example, the cuckoo (a conveniently musical bird, having a song of only two notes) appears, in the works of Vivaldi (*The Four Seasons*), Beethoven (Symphony No. 6, 'Pastoral'), Mahler (Symphony No. 1, 'Titan'). Delius quoted the bird verbatim (On Hearing the First Cuckoo in Spring). Other, more mechanical means were available to the enthusiastic composer, usually as adjuncts of the percussion department, including the wind machine (also known as the aeoliphone), a device involving a revolving sheet of silk, brushing against a wooden sounding board), coupled with a contraption for reproducing the sound of thunder (usually a large drum containing balls or stones). These were essentially theatrical sound effects which are nowadays done better by electronic reproductions, but were actually specified in the scores of some composers, like Richard Strauss in works such as the *Alpine Symphony* and *Don Quixote*.

Although this straightforward imitation of sounds is a rather crude way in which music can evoke non-musical images, composers have long striven to create impressions of people, places or dramatic situations by purely musical means, using vocal and instrumental resources to draw the listener into an imaginary place or situation. As early as the sixteenth century, for example, Clement Janequin wrote a number of descriptive vocal pieces (see Chapter 9). A great many composers since then have sought to communicate extra-musical scenes and emotions through their music. Let's take a well-known and much-loved example.

▶ Overture: *Hebrides* or 'Fingal's Cave', by Felix Mendelssohn (1809–47)

This is a concert overture, which is firmly founded on the sonata pattern as set out in Chapter 04. We can identify the structure of exposition, development, recapitulation and coda, but the work gives out more information than that. Mendelssohn was travelling in Scotland in 1829, when he conceived the idea of this work. He intended it to represent his musical impression of the beautiful but remote Hebrides islands, particularly Staffa, in which lies Fingal's Cave (the subtitle of the piece) with its legendary associations. The original version (1830) was called *The Lonely Island*, but the present title was adopted for the first performance in London in 1832. Although the work is given the title of 'Overture', it has an extra dimension in the form of musical tone painting, evoking the wild, windswept landscape, surrounded by an angry sea, with perhaps a hazardous boat trip as the only way to reach the islands.

But how does Mendelssohn achieve all this through purely musical means? Listen to the overture now. (If you do not already possess one, an album of Mendelssohn overtures would be a good addition to your basic collection. There are several reasonably-priced recordings currently available.)

There are no direct imitations of scene-setting sounds to convey the impression of 'blubber, seagulls and the tang of salted cod' that Mendelssohn described in a letter to his sister Fanny. Instead we find undulating tunes in the strings suggesting the sea, and timpani rolls accompanied by rapid passages on strings and high woodwind and brass denoting storms. When the thematic material is brought to a climax in the development section, we feel not only the musical excitement, but are transported into the eye of the storm. Mendelssohn is manipulating our imagination with his tonal pictures. But, how much of this imagery is in the music, and how much is suggested by the title and its connotations? If there was no title, would we still smell the ozone of the Hebrides, or would we be content to enjoy this as a fine concert overture in its own right?

Perhaps Mendelssohn is actually restricting our imaginative potential by telling us that this piece refers to a specific subject. Listeners may wish to construct images of their own making when enjoying a piece which is presented without a title. In his novel *Howard's End*, E.

M. Forster gives us an insight into the minds of different listeners at a concert:

> *It will be generally admitted that Beethoven's Fifth Symphony is the most sublime noise that has ever penetrated the ear of man. All sorts and conditions are satisfied by it. Whether you are like Mrs Munt, and tap surreptitiously when the tunes come – of course, not so as to disturb the others; or like Helen, who can see heroes and shipwrecks in the music's flood; or like Margaret, who can see only the music; or like Tibby, who is profoundly versed in counterpoint, and holds the full score open on his knee . . .*

Forster was primarily concerned with the foibles and pretensions of the middle-class characters he was describing, but he also gives us a summary of some of the perfectly valid ways in which we listen to music. Mrs Munt really only enjoys the main themes, probably not closely following the development sections. Helen is our romantic, who constructs extra-musical scenarios to fit otherwise abstract pieces, while the more prosaic Margaret enjoys only the purely musical experience. Poor Tibby, though the most knowledgeable listener, is so preoccupied with the technical aspects of the music that its emotional impact is lost on him.

▶ Beethoven's Symphony No. 6, 'Pastoral'

If the human mind is capable of producing such varied responses as these, then why should a composer choose to limit the imagination of the listener to a single idea, or set of images? Always remember that you, as the listener, are free to accept or reject such associations, and evaluate the music on your own terms. You can listen to a piece as pure music, or construct your own images like Helen, in the extract above. But it can be fun to go along with the composer if you feel like it, and allow yourself to share the musical images that are suggested to you. Beethoven's glorious 'Pastoral' symphony (1808), is an exciting example to try. The scenes depicted in each movement are fully described, and, as you can see below, correspond closely to a conventional symphonic structure (in brackets):

1 'Awakening of happy feelings on arrival in the country' (quick first movement)

2 'Scene by the Brook' (slow movement)

3 'Merry Gathering of Peasants' (scherzo)

4 & 5 'Thunderstorm and Shepherd's Song – Thanksgiving after the Storm' (finale).

Beethoven claimed that this was 'more an expression of feeling than a painting', but the work nevertheless contains numerous evocative devices, such as the birdsong in the second movement (named in the score as cuckoo, nightingale and quail). The crude rustic dance-music in the third movement, and, of course, the thunderstorm, all paint the clearest of pictures, but all this would be nothing without the sublime melodies which make the symphony one of the most memorable works in the orchestral repertoire. Without the scenery, this would still be great music, and can be enjoyed as such, but, if you take the whole package, an extra dimension is offered.

▶ Listen now to **Track 5** on the CD: Beethoven, Symphony No. 6, *Pastoral,* first movement, 'Awakening of Happy Feeling on Arriving in the Countryside'. Beethoven favours simplicity in this evocation of rural bliss. There is no attempt at direct imitation of rustic sounds, and all the effects mentioned above: the birdsong, rustic dance and thunderstorm, appear in subsequent movements. Here we have a perfect example of Beethoven's avowed 'expression of feeling', which is confirmed in the title. The first subject, which dominates the movement (in **sonata** form), begins immediately, giving the effect of a curtain drawing back to reveal an idyllic vista. It's a short theme, but has great strength and most of the movement is constructed from it. The melody is repeated throughout the whole orchestra, then, after a brief transition, the second subject is introduced. The modesty of the new theme contrasts with the expansiveness of the first, and we are presented with a smooth, sinewy eight-note figure, the first five of which form a descending phrase. The last three notes of this phrase are repeated, giving the impression of continuous motion, as fundamental as the regenerating cycle of nature itself. Beethoven gives us this figure in two slightly different melodic forms, alternating with each other, but always maintaining the impetus of the music.

In between the two main subjects, there is an important linking passage in this movement, which grows out of the tail end of the opening theme. Again we have a five-note phrase, but it differs from the second subject, being much more insistent. Listen carefully for this figure; it begins with two short notes, followed by three longer ones. It might help to sing the rhythm of this phrase, which goes: 'tiddle-om-pom-POM' (try it!), and this recurs in the development section in a slightly altered form. Beethoven changes the emphasis so that the second and third notes are shorter than the other three and the phrase has a stronger impact, becoming 'POM-tiddle-om-pom'. Where have we heard this before? Think back to the grand opening theme and take away the first three notes of the melody, concentrating on the second bar only. There is the phrase in its original form. Beethoven takes this seed and allows it to grow organically, gaining strength throughout the piece, and binding together the different sections. Please listen to this track again, paying particular attention to these linking passages, and note how Beethoven uses this fragment of his main theme to maintain unity and momentum throughout the movement.

Now, if you use your skills to listen below the surface, you will hear some very basic harmonies (**tonic** and **dominant**, if you want the technical terms), which form the basis of many simple tunes and are most marked in the country-dance, which appears in the third movement. So in various subtle ways, Beethoven conveys the impression of his feelings on arriving in the countryside, and hints at some of the delights to follow in the rest of the symphony. It is worth mentioning the work was completed at Heilingenstadt, where he had agonized over his oncoming deafness eight years earlier (if you want to know more about Beethoven's early life, read page 68, in Part Two of this book). This movement seems to indicate that the composer was able to enjoy the beauties of nature, despite his tragic condition. Nevertheless, the Pastoral Symphony is a dramatic piece, and the storm (fourth movement) could be interpreted as Beethoven shaking his fist at the heavens in anger and frustration. Joy of life does finally prevail and the symphony closes with a happy song. For now though, listen once more to this glorious music, and see if you can put together all the elements discussed above. With careful listening, you will discover even more delights in this deceptively simple, but profoundly effective work.

It should be mentioned, briefly, that an earlier attempt by Beethoven at descriptive music produced a less than sublime result. The inventor Johann Maelzel, better known for patenting the **metronome**, of which Beethoven was an early advocate, had constructed a mechanical device he called an 'orchestrion', and he commissioned

Beethoven to write a piece for the machine. The result was the so-called 'Battle Symphony' or, more correctly, *Wellington's Victory – The Battle of Vittoria*, composed in 1813. Basically, the British forces are represented by the tune 'Rule Britannia', and the French by a ditty called 'Malbrouk', which dies away after a 'Storm March' featuring cannon effects and mechanical drums. 'God Save the King' signals the British victory, and is developed as a **fugue**. The orchestrion, also called the 'panharmonicon', seems to have been the forerunner of the fairground organ that was eventually taken to America by its inventor, who apparently met with some success. Beethoven did not write any further pieces for the machine.

Impressionism

The epitome of musical sound painting is to be found in the works of Claude Debussy (1862–1918), Maurice Ravel (1875–1937), and other composers who have been dubbed Impressionists. This term was employed by critics rather than the musicians themselves, who resisted such labelling. Nevertheless, parallels can be drawn between the work of certain composers and the techniques of the well-known group of painters including Monet, Cézanne and Renoir, who softened the definition of their images to evoke an impression of the subject, rather than an accurate reproduction. Returning to maritime subject matter, a major specimen of this type of Impressionist tone painting is Debussy's orchestral work, *La Mer* (1905), subtitled *Three Symphonic Sketches of the Sea*. The orchestra is employed in a very different manner from the rather clearly defined roles observed by the composers in Austro-German tradition from Haydn to Bruckner. Instrumental groupings are brought into play for the effect, their tone colours mixed as on a painter's palette. The evocation of the sea is achieved, on a surface level, through musical devices such as timpani rolls, harp **glissandi** and rippling passages on strings and woodwind, all of which are instantly recognizable as musical shorthand for the wind and the waves. Ultimately, though, we receive an impression of the emotions aroused by the seascape rather than a catalogue of sound effects.

The three movements or 'sketches' in *La Mer* are titled: 'From Dawn to Midday on the Sea', 'Play of the Waves' and 'Dialogue of the Wind and the Sea'. At the end of the third section, snatches of the thematic material from the opening of the work are heard, providing an element of unity in the absence of a strict formal structure, in a way mirroring the cyclic nature of the sea itself. The final section contains the most animated music, with quicksilver brass parts, and dynamics swelling and dipping until the final climactic close. The work could possibly be thought of as a symphony in three movements, with the meditative first section followed by a scherzo-like interlude, and completed with a rousing finale. But this piece has moved a long way from the eighteenth-century symphonic form we encountered in Haydn and Mozart.

The majority of the audience at one early performance of this music in Paris, were not prepared to make allowances for the new idioms and concepts that were presented to them. The occasion became the focus of a violent dispute between Debussy's supporters and antagonists. Shouts of 'Bravo' alternated with hisses and catcalls, and a stormy ten-minute demonstration erupted after the performance. New music requires an adjustment in focus from the audience as well as the musicians. Boundaries of expectation have to be revised to accommodate the unfamiliar. Those members of Debussy's audience who expected the music to proceed along conventional lines would naturally have been disappointed.

Listening to *La Mer*

▶ **CD track 6, Debussy's *La Mer*, 2nd movement, *Jeux de Vagues* (Play of the Waves)**

We are going to listen to this music principally for its sensual imagery, but let's also consider how Debussy creates these sound pictures. As you listen, think particularly about orchestral texture, that is, how the different instruments and sections of the orchestra (particularly strings, woodwind and brass) are used.

Questions to consider:
- Can you hear instruments that you would not expect to find in the orchestras of Beethoven or Mendelssohn?

- Are the instruments used as soloists or in combinations of groups?

- Are there many discernible melodies and, if so, which instruments are featured?

- Compare this music with Mendelssohn's Hebridean seascape, discussed on page 24. Is the orchestra used in the same way?

- Does the piece work, **a** as a piece of music, and **b** as a tone painting? Would the image of the coruscating waves have been conjured up in your mind if you had not known about the title of the work?

Debussy's orchestra is essentially the symphonic model as used by Beethoven and Mendelssohn (with a couple of additions, notably harp and **celesta**), but the way he employs the instruments in *La Mer* is radically different from anything we have studied so far. Rather than main themes we have little fragments of melody, which are passed from instrument to instrument. The woodwind are prominent at the beginning of the movement, particularly the flutes (Debussy seems to have had a particular affection for this instrument). Flutes give way rapidly to a trumpet (softened by a mute placed in the bell of the instrument), and a solo oboe, playing a brief jittery melody, with rapid, repeated notes. Unlike earlier symphonic writing, the strings do not dominate the **ensemble**, but play an equal part with the woodwind and brass in the orchestral mix. The trumpets, thanks partly to technology in shape of the valve (see page 30) are now capable of playing **chromatic** passages, and are alternated with woodwind to add extra colour to Debussy's sound picture. The harp is also used in a non-traditional way, adding atmospheric **glissandi**, as mentioned earlier, but, at the close of the movement there is a particularly beautiful and haunting interplay between the harp and solo flute, which suggests a temporary calm settling on the capricious sea.

I hope you will agree that Debussy achieved his aim in an original and unique way, with subtle effects, rather than cliché'd imitation. It is difficult to listen to *La Mer* simply as pure music, without reference to the sea, having thought about the extra-musical rationale of the piece. However, I think it can be said that this work satisfies all the elements of a good musical experience in terms of form and construction. It might be best to conclude that the sea provided the inspiration for Debussy to create a musical masterpiece, and leave it at that.

I would submit that this type of music should be listened to in a less than analytical way. It would not be helpful to count bars, or to identify themes with the idea of following their development. It would be better to open your ears and mind, and allow yourself to drift with the musical tide. After listening to the piece a few times you may begin to discern the sun glistening on the waves, hear the cries of sea birds and feel the force of the wind and the sea-spray on your face.

Debussy was aware of the art and artifice of the images he was creating and their impact on the imaginative sensibilities of his audience. In 1903, two years before the completion of *La Mer*, he wrote to his friend André Messager:

> *My seascapes might be studio landscapes, but I have an endless store of memories and, to my mind, they are worth more than the reality, whose beauty often deadens thought.*

He reminds us that it is an essentially human product that we are listening to and evaluating. Through Debussy's music we can exercise the power of our own memories, and allow our imagination to create pleasing images, to complement the sensual realities of the orchestral sounds.

08 musical narrative: telling a story

In this chapter you will learn:

● about programme music, the symphonic poem and music drama, a term coined by Richard Wagner to describe his enormous musical concepts

● about the story as well as the music, in our third case study: Berlioz's *Symphonie Fantastique*.

As we have seen, there has always been a desire in some composers to extend the range of expression of their music into other realms, and we have been considering examples of pieces inspired mainly by natural phenomena. In the nineteenth century, some Romantic composers began to build a poetic or narrative element into their music. Franz Liszt (1811–86), for example, suggested that a written preface should be provided with a piece of instrumental music, setting out the composer's extra-musical inspiration 'to guard the listener against a wrong poetical interpretation'. This is something we have not come across before: the composer is telling us that there is a right and wrong way to listen to his music. Liszt believed that there was an essential inner connection between music and poetic art. He thought that music should always pursue a path towards the ultimate goal of a perfect fusion of these two elements. It would, therefore, be necessary for the listener to know the details of the composer's extra-musical influences in order to experience the music to the fullest extent.

Programme music

The term 'programme music', was coined by Liszt to describe the kind of work that was informed by a literary or narrative idea, as opposed to 'absolute' or 'abstract' music, which relies on a formal system of repeated and contrasted themes to balance and unify its structure.

One of the most interesting examples of this type of programme music is provided by Hector Berlioz (1803–69) in his *Symphonie Fantastique*, which was completed in 1830. The romantic, young composer had fallen for the Irish actress Harriet Smithson, who had been in Paris playing Ophelia in a touring version of *Hamlet*. Harriet, whom Berlioz eventually married, became the inspiration for the programme of this work, with a wildly romantic and partially autobiographical storyline, which begins as follows:

A young musician of morbid sensibility and abundant imagination, in the depths of despair because of hopeless love, has poisoned himself with opium. Not having taken a lethal dose, he falls into a deep sleep accompanied by weird dreams. His sensations, emotions and memories, as they pass through his affected mind, are transformed into musical images and ideas. The beloved one herself becomes to him a melody, a recurrent theme (idée fixe) which haunts him continually.

Let's now follow the story, as published in Berlioz's notes to the original score, listening to the music as we go.

Berlioz

▶ Case study 3 – Berlioz, *Symphonie Fantastique*
First movement – Reveries, passions

The story
First, the artist remembers the weariness of the soul, the indefinable longing, the sombre melancholia and the baseless depressions and elations that he felt before he saw the object of his adoration. Then, the volcanic love with which she instantly inspired in him, his jealous rages, his rediscovered love, his religious consolations.

The music
After such a detailed preamble, it comes as a surprise to find that this movement is constructed in conventional **sonata form**. The *idée fixe*, representing the loved one, makes an early appearance in the first violins, with the flute added. It is a distinctive little tune, the first four notes are the constituents of a common chord, basic notes which can be played on a bugle, natural harmonics which communicate in the clearest and most fundamental way. This series of notes is repeated at a lower pitch, and the tune is rounded off over the next few bars. The first movement, the longest in the symphony, contains a

significant amount of development of this theme, which serves to implant the *idée fixe* in our musical mind's eye. We are being unconsciously prepared for its reappearance.

Second movement – A Ball

The story
At a ball, in the midst of a noisy, brilliant fête, the artists sees his beloved again.

The music
Berlioz rather extravagantly decided that two harps should introduce this movement, which is a lively waltz tune initially led by the strings. The *idée fixe* suddenly appears, in the woodwind (flute and oboe), while the waltz rhythm continues. Here, the theme intrudes upon an unrelated melody, rather than growing organically out of the subject matter, as in the previous movement. The musical effect successfully illustrates the text, creating the effect of glimpsing a familiar face across a crowded ballroom. The *idée fixe* briefly and quietly reappears, whispered by a clarinet, before the orchestra brings the dance to its close.

Third movement – In the Country

The story
On a summer evening in the country, the artist hears two herders calling each other with their shepherd melodies. The pastoral duet in such surroundings, the gentle rustle of the trees softly swayed by the wind, some reasons for hope which had come to his knowledge recently – all unite to fill his heart with a rare tranquillity and lend brighter colours to his fancies. But his beloved appears anew, spasms contract his heart, and he is filled with dark premonition. What if she should prove faithless? Only one of the shepherds resumes his rustic tune. The sun sets. Far away there is rumbling thunder – solitude – silence.

The music
The two shepherds are represented by oboe and cor anglais (a double-reed woodwind instrument related to the oboe, but with a deeper pitch). Their melancholy dialogue gives way to a slow movement of great beauty and tranquillity. Eventually this mood is interrupted by the appearance of the *idée fixe*, whereupon the music becomes agitated, dark rumblings are heard from the timpani and a storm threatens, reminiscent of

Beethoven's 'Pastoral', but, unlike that symphony, the storm does not develop. Instead, it dies away, with the single shepherd intoning the now lonely tune to end the movement in a spirit of grim foreboding, underlined by soft but ominous murmurings from the timpani.

▶ Track 7: Fourth movement – March to the Scaffold

The story
The artist dreams he has killed his loved one, that he is condemned to death and led to his execution. A march, now gloomy and ferocious, now solemn and brilliant, accompanies the procession. Noisy outbursts are followed without pause by the heavy sound of measured footsteps. Finally, like a last thought of love, the *idée fixe* appears for a moment, to be cut off by the fall of the axe.

The cornet

Berlioz was one of the first composers to use the new *cornet à pistons*, the valved cornet used in brass bands today. The invention of the valve meant that the instrument was now capable of playing all the notes in all keys, not just the **natural** harmonics obtainable on a non-valved or natural instrument. Although similar in pitch and range to the trumpet, the cornet has a conical bore (the trumpet, except for the flared 'bell' section, is cylindrical), which produces a more mellow sound. The greater agility of the new instrument is reflected in the nature of the fanfare in the *Symphonie Fantastique*. As we heard in *La Mer*, the modern trumpet is also equipped with valves and is capable of executing rapid and complex passages.

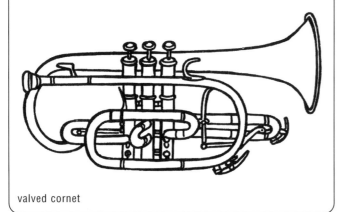

valved cornet

The music
In this movement, Berlioz uses the orchestra in a particularly imaginative and evocative way. Appropriately, drum tattoos are the first sounds to be heard, as the prisoner is led through the crowd to the scaffold. The rhythmic patterns of the drums are gradually taken up by the orchestra as the solemn march progresses and the nervous tension builds. Listen below the surface and you will hear an insistent, quick-moving bassoon beneath the orchestral chords. The condemned man hears the crowd gossiping and chattering as he is led to his execution. Fanfares erupt from the cornets.

But they are fanfares without nobility, their solemnity splintered into quick-moving, fleeting tunes, which suddenly give way to the *idée fixe*, heard this time on the clarinet. The crash of the blade is followed by the dull thud of the severed head falling into the basket, supplied by the double-basses, played **pizzicato** (plucked). Loud rolls on the side drums and repeated chords from the full orchestra signify the approbation of the mob as the execution is performed. It is worth remembering that this symphony was written within living memory of the French Revolution, and that Berlioz was of a generation that grew up with stories of the heroic struggle ringing in its ears. Little wonder, then, that he should choose a public beheading as the dramatic climax of his revolutionary new symphony. But there is more to come. Having killed his heroine, and paid the ultimate price, there is nothing left for the artist to contemplate in his dreams but an eternity of torment in the fires of Hell.

▶ Track 8: Fifth movement – The Witches' Sabbath

The story
The artist sees himself at a witches' sabbath surrounded by a fearful crowd of spectres, sorcerers and monsters of every kind, united for his burial. He hears unearthly sounds, groans, shrieks of laughter, distant cries, to which others seem to respond! The melody of his beloved is heard, but it has lost its character of nobility and reserve. Instead, it is now an ignoble dance tune, trivial and grotesque. It is she who comes to the sabbath! A shout of joy greets her arrival. She joins the diabolical orgy. There follows the funeral knell, burlesque of the Dies Irae; the dance of the witches; the dance and the Dies Irae combined.

The music

Berlioz has given us a sketch-plan of the music in this final movement. Compare this description with that of the first movement and you will see how precise the musical language has become. The opening programme refers to 'indefinable longing', 'volcanic love' and 'delirious sufferings', descriptions of emotions which the composer intends to evoke in the course of the first movement. The notes to the final movement, on the other hand, tell of the alteration in the character of the *idée fixe* (now a trivial dance tune), the introduction of the Dies Irae (literally, 'Day of Wrath') theme, and the combination of the two themes as a finale.

The music and the drama are now much more closely related and interdependent than they were in the sonata-form first movement. It just remains to fill in some of the musical details of this fascinating final movement. Listen for the following:

1 The ominous movement in the lower strings which presages the strange things which are about to happen.

2 The transformed *idée fixe*, now a manic waltz, introduced by a shrill, high-pitched clarinet, accompanied by burbling bassoons. The tune is gradually taken up by the full orchestra.

3 After the bells, the Dies Irae, an old plainsong melody, traditionally part of the Requiem Mass, is intoned by the lower woodwind and brass.

4 The *idée fixe* and the Dies Irae are played together. Berlioz chooses the **fugato**, a form which is more commonly associated with composers of an earlier age (see Chapter 09) to develop and combine the two themes. Basically, this is a linear form of composition. That is to say that it involves two or more lines of melody which move independently. This means that the thematic material appears in the different lines at different times, and often appears as though one part is chasing another through the piece. This, of course, fits in capitally with the image of the witches' sabbath, with its orgiastic revelry.

Berlioz piles on the heat with some exciting details like the off-beat (syncopated) brass intrusions, which spur on the fugue. At one stage the violins are instructed to play *col lengo* (literally 'with the wood'), which involves turning the bow upside down and striking the strings with the stick, producing a clattering sound (dancing skeletons?), adding to the bizarre, other-worldly effect. The movement, and the symphony, ends with a thunderous coda, leaving a silence which can be filled only with applause. Berlioz knew how to manipulate the emotional responses of his audience.

The programme and the music seem so perfectly matched in this symphony that it comes as a surprise to learn that much of the music had been used by the composer before. The 'March to the Scaffold', for example, had originally been part of an early, unperformed opera *Les Francs-Juges* (The Judges of the Secret Court), and the *idée fixe* melody itself had been part of a cantata, *Herminie*, which Berlioz had composed in 1828 in an unsuccessful attempt to win the Prix de Rome competition. None of this detracts from the achievement of the *Symphonie Fantastique*, however. Berlioz certainly wasn't the first composer to recycle musical ideas, and the symphony is unified by the double bond of music and drama. The programme and the music become inseparable in the mind of the listener, a successful demonstration of the composer's avowed aim of 'the organisation of musical moments around a single subject, at once musical and dramatic'.

As we have seen, this work can be properly described as a symphony, despite the fact that the programme provides an extra-musical element in its dramatic underpinning. The sonata-form first movement and juxtaposition of fast and slow movements can still be related to the symphonic tradition of Mozart and Haydn. It was Liszt who took the next logical step in the development of programme music when he abandoned the traditional symphonic framework, replacing it with a single-movement work, the structure of which was, theoretically at least, determined by the 'poetic' subject matter of its programme.

The symphonic poem

The idea of the symphonic poem was that a theme representing the 'poetic' (non-musical) subject could be altered and developed progressively to suggest a narrative flow. In a way, this is a similar concept to the changes made by Berlioz to his *idée fixe* as the *Symphonie Fantastique* progressed. The major difference is that, in Berlioz's work, each movement introduced new themes, with the *idée fixe* as a recurring feature, whereas, in a

Liszt symphonic poem the theme and its gradual metamorphosis provides all the dramatic momentum of the piece. Liszt wrote 12 symphonic poems on various themes, including *Les Préludes* (after a poem by Lamartine, first performed in 1854), *Tasso* (inspired by a poem by Byron, first performed 1849) and *Mazeppa* (based on Victor Hugo's poem about a cossack leader, premiered in 1854). These works are not heard all that frequently in the concert hall, but there are good recordings available.

Various composers dabbled with the symphonic or tone-poem as it was often called, in the nineteenth and early twentieth centuries, but the one man who became most closely associated with the form was Richard Strauss (1864–1949). No relation of the Viennese waltzing family, Richard was the son of a horn player in the Munich Court Opera orchestra. In his hands the symphonic poem reached the heights of realistic, literal depiction. We have already heard his name associated with early mechanical instruments like the aeoliophone (see Chapter 5) and he certainly had a penchant for vivid sound pictures. In *Don Quixote* (1897) we actually hear the wind turning the sails of the windmill at which the Don is tilting. We also hear the bleating of sheep in the same piece (flutter-tongued horns) and cowbells in the *Alpine Symphony* (1915).

In common with some of the other Romantic composers (see Chapter 12), Strauss had a tendency towards autobiography. *A Hero's Life* (*Ein Heldenleben*) appeared in 1898 (no prizes for guessing the name of the hero), and the *Domestic Symphony* (1903), contained a sequence representing the bathing of a baby, and a sourly harmonized passage meant to describe the carping of Strauss's critics. *Till Eulenspiegel's Merry Pranks* is good fun, based on an old German folk-story about a lovable rogue. He is represented musically by two themes, which both appear at the beginning of the piece. A short, quirky passage is first heard on the violins, followed by a longer motif played by the horn. Both themes have a humorous character, involving a good deal of agility, the horn part being particularly difficult to play, because of the huge range between the top and bottom notes demanded by the composer. These themes are modified as the work progresses and Till's pranks eventually lead to the gallows. Compare the execution scene with the *Symphonie Fantastique* – there are some similarities, although the *Till* storyline has the hero posthumously raised to his true status as a popular legend. Strauss, in

common with many of his countrymen, was preoccupied to a great extent with the idea of the heroic figure, and this found musical expression in *Also Sprach Zarathustra* (1896) based on a work by the philosopher and poet Friedrich Nietzsche (1844–1900). Film fans will remember the portentous opening of this piece in the science-fiction epic, *2001 – A Space Odyssey*.

Wagner's music-dramas

Strauss took the programme idea to the extremes of realism in purely instrumental terms, but he did not solve the fundamental problem of producing an accurate portrayal of dramatic events in music. No matter how detailed the programme, or how many realistic devices are brought into play, a symphonic poem can still be listened to, and enjoyed, as a piece of pure music, without any reference by the listener to the extra-musical narrative. A different, and perhaps more successful, solution to this problem had already been found by Richard Wagner (1813–83), when he came up with the idea of 'music-drama'. Wagner's musical inspiration came from earlier instrumental works, especially the symphonies of Beethoven. The Ninth Symphony particularly fascinated him, with the choral setting of Schiller's

Wagner

poem *Ode to Joy* in its final movement, which he rightly saw as an extension of the scope of the symphony and a milestone in symphonic music (see pages 70–1). He rejected the idea of programme music, and instead formulated a concept of synthesizing music, drama, poetry and the visual arts in a continuous narrative work marking each character and idea with its own musical theme, or **Leitmotiv** (literally 'leading theme', a similar idea to Berlioz's *idée fixe*).

Wagner never thought on a small scale, and the realization of his ideas took the form of 13 large-scale music-dramas, of which the last seven conform most closely to his philosophy of composition. These are (the dates are of completion, not first performance): *Tristan and Isolde* (1859), *The Mastersingers* (1867), *The Ring of the Nibelung* (1854–74, comprising *The Rhinegold*, *The Valkyries*, *Siegfried* and *The Twilight of the Gods*) and *Parsifal* (1882). The new technique allowed Wagner to explore his musical and poetic ideas at great length without a loss of continuity, and most of these works take several hours to perform. He saw his music as a continuation of the great German musical tradition and mainly chose Germanic folk-stories as the subject matter for his music-dramas, writing the **libretti** (words to be sung) himself in a style based on German medieval poetry.

The Ring of the Nibelung

The *Ring* tetralogy is Wagner's most complex and ambitious work, composed over a period of 20 years and finally staged in its entirety at the new purpose-built *Festspielhaus* at Bayreuth in 1876. *Götterdämmerung* (The Twilight of the Gods) is the final opera in the cycle and in it, events are finally resolved in a cataclysmic finale. The plot is convoluted and the gigantic work is unified by the **Leitmotives**, which can identify a character, emotion or idea, and are carried through all four operas.

A brief version of the story

Based on Nordic and Teutonic myths, the tale of the Ring is centred on a hoard of magic gold, secreted in the depths of the Rhine, which was watched over by the Rhine-maidens, who dwelt beneath the waves, unseen by most mortal eyes. The Nibelungs are a subterranean species with a great interest in mineral wealth, and one of their number, Alberich, contrives to steal the gold from the Rhine-maidens. The god Wotan, having contracted two giants to build a palace, seeks an alternative payment for this, rather than forsaking his sister Freia, who provides the golden apples, which prevent the gods from aging. Wotan tricks Albericht into giving up the gold, and gives it to the giants in payment for the palace, which is called Valhalla. But the stolen gold carries with it a curse, and while the ring fashioned from the gold grants its wearer unlimited power, no good will ever come of it until it is returned to the Rhine-maidens. Wotan, struck with a sense of foreboding, wanders the earth seeking a solution to this problem, calling upon his daughters the Valkyries, a species of airborne horseback warriors.

After a liaison between brother and sister Siegmund and Sieglinde, one of the Valkyries, Brünnhilde, tries to prevent the slaying of Siegmund in a duel with his rival for her affections, which has been approved by the god of justice. Wotan intervenes, allows Siegmund to die and removes Brünnhilde to a remote mountain top, surrounded by a circle of fire as a punishment for her disobedience. She can only be rescued by a man who does not know the meaning of fear. The result of the union between Siegmund and Sieglinde is Siegfried, who has been brought up in the woods as an orphan (his mother having died after his birth) by Mime, brother of Alberich. Mime wants to retrieve the gold from the remaining giant, who, having killed his brother, is now transformed by the power of the ring into a dragon. After re-forging the magic sword left for him by his father, Siegfried slays the dragon, and proceeds, guided by his friends the birds to find Brünnhilde, defying even the mighty Wotan on his way. On finding the lovely Valkyrie he strides through the fiery cordon to waken her in the time-honoured heroic fashion – with a kiss. She agrees to become his wife, even though this will mean the loss of her immortality, and they exchange vows of love with each other.

Leaving the now mortal Brünnhilde with the Ring as a symbol of their betrothal, Siegfried sets out with his magic sword and Brünnhilde's horse Grane, in search of the noble and heroic adventures for which he believes himself destined. It is at this point that we join him.

▶ 'Siegfried's Rhine Journey' from *Götterdämmerung* by Wagner

Listen now to track 9 on the CD, Wagner 'Siegfried's Rhine Journey' from *Götterdämmerung* (the Twilight of the Gods). It is dawn, and the music begins with quiet long notes in the lower strings until the horns play the first four notes of Siegfried's theme. The hero has a horn about him at all times, sometimes appearing to sound it on stage, but more often being accompanied by the instrument when he features in the narrative. His theme is heard in full about two minutes into the extract, and is immediately followed by a plaintive clarinet phrase representing Brünnhilde's love. This is identifiable by the turn (or *grupetto* in Italian), which is a strong part of the melody. The turn is simply a little decorative figure, consisting of the notes above and below the principal note quickly alternated. It is a familiar device, but used most effectively here to suggest feminine beauty and love. Play the beginning of the recording again, and listen carefully to the strong horn theme (Siegfried), followed by the softer, more decorative clarinet melody (Brünnhilde), until you are sure you can identify them.

Swirling violin figures remind us of the ever-present Rhine, and then the Rhine-maidens motive is briefly heard. This first appeared many hours of music earlier in the first opera in the cycle, *The Rhinegold*, and the sighing two-note motive suggests the words 'Rhine-gold, Rhine-gold'. Siegfried's theme is then announced loudly and aggressively by the full orchestra, underlining his power as possessor of the Ring. His horn call appears as a solo, suggesting distance, and is answered again by Brünnhilde's theme, this time on the bass clarinet (notice the difference in tone-quality, the lower instrument seemingly echoing through the depths of the mountains). The Siegfried music is then picked up and developed in a piece of triumphantly confident orchestral writing, which swirls along like the fast-flowing Rhine itself. One other theme is heard in this short piece, and that is an upward motive, progressing in steps (part of a **scale**) in alternating long and short notes. This represents an ominous warning from the goddess Erda, the spirit of Mother Earth, issuing a reminder of the curse of the Ring and a portent of cataclysmic events to follow.

The conclusion of the story

By various devices, Siegfried is duped into betraying Brünnhilde by the evil Hagen (who is related to Alberich), and is eventually killed by him. The former Valkyrie mounts her horse for the last time, and rides to her death on Siegfried's funeral pyre. As a great wave washes over the scene, the Rhine-maidens take back the Ring, pulling Hagen down to a watery grave. Valhalla is consumed in flames and the gods are destroyed, as the Curse of the Ring is finally played out.

The moral themes of power, greed and corruption transcend the archaic subject matter in this gigantic work, and of course are as relevant today as ever. *The Ring* is undoubtedly Wagner's masterpiece, and I hope this tiny fragment will encourage you to look deeper into the detail of the cycle, and as its mysteries unfold you will become fascinated by this miracle of organization and the sublime music it contains.

Staging the music dramas

These productions were intended as serious examples of high art, rather than mere entertainment, as Wagner considered most operatic performances to be. He felt that opera had been marred by lapses of artistic taste in the choice of trivial subject matter, the artificiality of setpiece **arias** (songs) that disturbed the dramatic flow, and the domination of music over poetry. Wagner wanted his works to have an almost spiritual effect, completely fusing the various artistic elements to produce a morally and uplifting, quasi-religious experience. Through the patronage of the eccentric King Ludwig II of Bavaria, who was one of Wagner's greatest admirers, a special theatre was built at Bayreuth so that the great music-dramas could receive the best possible staging. Wagner designed this theatre himself, creating conditions he felt to be as near to ideal as possible so that his works could achieve the transcendental effect that he envisaged. The Festspielhaus (Festival Theatre) is still open every summer for performances of Wagner's works, and has become something of a shrine for the many devotees of the composer, who make the annual pilgrimage to Bayreuth. Despite the composer's grand theories of artistic synthesis, it is the music which makes his works so memorable. His magnificently innovative melody, harmony and orchestration guaranteed his musical immortality. The theories are little more than historical curiosities now, and, although he disliked the term, his works are enjoyed as operas, among the very greatest, but operas nevertheless. It's interesting to identify the Leitmotives and link them with the various characters and situations created by this remarkable man. Obviously, attending a live performance is the only way to experience all the dimensions of any opera, but a word of warning – a Wagner performance usually draws a capacity audience, so if you're thinking of going to one, book early to avoid disappointment! There are also many recordings and videos available of live and studio performances of Wagner's operas.

Wagner and the Nazis

It is hard to shake off the stigma of being Hitler's favourite composer, and some of Wagner's ideas were taken up and distorted by the Third Reich more than 50 years after his death. It must be admitted that Wagner did express some pretty obnoxious views about German nationalism and anti-semitism, though it should be noted that the first performance of his final opera *Parsifal* was given under the Jewish conductor Hermann Levi. The critic Ernest Newman described Wagner as 'pro-semite in practice'. But really, all this is superfluous. The music is the important element, surpassing all other con-siderations, and its greatness is now universally accepted. In 2001, the conductor Daniel Barenboim took the unprecedented step of performing Wagner's music in Israel, where it had always been banned. Barenboim had long wanted to do this, and when he heard a mobile phone ring *The Ride of the Valkyries*, was struck by the inconsistencies of the situation, in a place where such music could be heard on a mobile phone and even on the radio, but not in the concert hall. He made up his mind to include an excerpt from *Tristan and Isolde* as an encore after a concert of Schumann and Stravinsky. Before performing the piece, he consulted his audience and a 30-minute debate ensued, after which some members of the audience walked out. But, despite this, the piece was played and received a standing ovation. Although there were repercussions from some prominent figures, including the prime minister, an important precedent had been set. The overall acceptance of the work by the audience showed that music has the power to overcome even the most profound human injustices.

Exploring the various processes of story-telling in music has led us, through the mixture of music and poetry in Wagner, to opera. We have moved from the programme symphony and symphonic poem, in which the importance of the extra-musical story is debatable, to a form which begins with, and cannot exist without, the story. There will be more about the development of opera in Part Two.

music for stage and screen

In this chapter you will learn:

- that music is often conceived as an integral part of other media, and we look at some of the ways this can happen, in the worlds of theatre, film and television.

Ballet

Ballet was another fruitful medium for musical expression. Early dramatic performances, particularly in France and Italy, featured a mixture of dance sequences as well as spoken and sung passages (the English equivalents were known as **masques**). Eventually, these separated into opera, ballet and drama as we know them today. A well-known practitioner of the first two of these forms was Jean-Baptiste Lully (1632–87), whom we will meet again in Chapter 08. Lully was a dancer as well as a musician, and composed a large number of ballets for the court of Louis XIV, as well as 15 operas (which included ballet numbers), plus a small amount of instrumental and church music.

The Russians later developed a taste for the ballet, and chief among their nineteenth-century composers was Peter Ilyich Tchaikovsky (1840–93) whose three ballets contain some of the best-known and best-loved music in the world. Most people would recognize some of the tunes from *Swan Lake* (1876), *Sleeping Beauty* (1889) and *Nutcracker* (1891–2). Snatches from these works have often been used in television advertisements and broadcasts of various kinds as 'background' music. Taken out of context, the extra-musical significance of the ballet themes disappears. Tchaikovsky arranged the music from *Swan Lake* and *Nutcracker* into orchestral suites which are played as concert items, with a series of short numbers following one another in quick succession. The narrative element is all but lost in this process.

Russian ballet reached its creative pinnacle in the hands of the impresario Sergei Diaghilev (1872–1929), who commissioned works from a number of young composers, including Igor Stravinsky (1882–1971) and Maurice Ravel (1875–1937). Diaghilev always hired the best choreographers, dancers and stage designers for his productions, people whose names became famous, like Fokine, Pavlova, Nijinsky and Picasso. In a way he could be said to have had a grand conception of total art in a Wagnerian sense, though the resulting music was very different. Works like *Firebird* (1910), *Petrushka* (1911) and *The Rite of Spring* (1913) from Stravinsky, and Ravel's *Daphnis et Chloé* (1912) were considered to be the last word in modernity. The *Rite of Spring* received an even worse reception in Paris than *La Mer* had a few years earlier (see Chapter 05). Fights broke out between the composer's supporters, and antagonists (the majority), who were outraged by what they felt were uncouth and primitive sounds.

The Rite of Spring by Stravinsky

The story (from an idea of Stravinsky's) is of a pagan

Debussy and Stravinsky

fragment of a Lithuanian folk-tune. This part, played in the instrument's higher register, is not typical of the piece. There are no further folk melodies, in fact there are no sustained melodies at all. On the entry of the strings, pizzicato at first, then thunderously repeating a huge chord with various off-beat accents, the mood changes, and a series of wild dances begins. Themes are short and strongly rhythmic, and their effect is achieved by repetition and changing orchestration. These rhythmic patterns and their development provide the basic structure of the piece. There is also an exhilarating sense of forward momentum. We are carried along, breathless, by the energy of the primal forces that have been released.

All this must have sounded very strange to a 1913 audience. There are no contrasting themes as in sonata form, no *idées fixes* or Leitmotivs to provide musical signposts. Nor is there a scheme of harmonic organization which leads comfortingly back to a 'home' key. Stravinsky combined notes and chords in a way that seemed cacophonous, and the violence of the rhythms seemed almost indecent. The piece also contains many technical problems for the musicians, which must have adversely affected some of the early performances. Today's orchestral players, familiar with Stravinsky's music, have conquered these difficulties, and the *Rite* is often performed as a concert item.

So, if this work is now more commonly heard as an orchestral piece than a ballet, we come back to the original question of the extent to which music can tell the story. Stravinsky was quite content to let the music speak for itself: 'I have never tried in my stage works, to make the music illustrate the action, or the action the music . . . The *Rite* exists as a piece of music, first and last'. He went on to say that the subject matter was a 'pretext' for the music, and no more. But, with a piece of music as powerful and evocative as this, and knowing its history, we have preconceived notions about what the piece represents. I wonder whether anyone enjoys a concert performance of *The Rite of Spring* without visualizing or even feeling something of its 'pretext' of pagan ritual and sacrifice. The harsh and violent nature of the music is indisputable, however you approach it. This can't be listened to as a lullaby! In any event we are listening to a major innovation in musical history. In Part Two we shall see how Stravinsky played a pivotal part in the development of music in the twentieth century.

ritual in which the earth, and its fecundity, is worshipped, culminating in the sacrifice of a young girl to the god of spring. The work is in two parts corresponding to the two sections of the story. Part one, 'The Adoration of the Earth', includes dances to celebrate the coming of spring, and the procession of the elders to the place of sacrifice. Part two, 'The Sacrifice', centres on the victim herself and the ritual culminating in the sacrifice, in which the girl dances herself to death. Stravinsky provided startling music to match his own violent storyline and in doing so broke new ground in harmony, orchestration, and, most significantly, rhythm.

'The Adoration of the Earth'

If we take a closer look at the first five minutes or so of music, we can get an idea of just how different and disturbing this piece must have seemed to its first audience. The opening section, 'Auguries of Spring' is the most impressionistic in its scene-setting, representing Stravinsky's idea of 'the awakening of nature, the scratching, gnawing, wriggling of birds and insects'. The instruments of the woodwind section of the orchestra blend their voices to produce this effect, but first we hear a lone bassoon, playing a plaintive melody which is a

Incidental music

Music which accompanies drama is generally known as incidental music. Throughout the history of the theatre, from ancient times to the present day, music has been an important adjunct to the drama on stage. Shakespeare demanded musical interludes and songs in his plays, and many Elizabethan dramatists wrote masques. Henry Purcell (1659–95) wrote music for more than 40 plays, and we have already encountered William Boyce (see Chapter 3), whose 'symphonys' began life as theatrical pieces.

This sort of incidental music is normally confined to overtures, interludes and perhaps one or two songs, which have survived in the main as concert pieces. Distinguished examples include Beethoven's music for *Egmont* (1810), Schubert's for *Rosamunde* (1823) and Mendelssohn's for *A Midsummer Night's Dream* (1826 and 1842). In this last case, the 17-year-old Mendelssohn produced a remarkable overture which manages to sketch out the whole play in a matter of 12 minutes or so. Briefly, this is how it goes:

Overture: *A Midsummer Night's Dream* by Mendelssohn

Four gentle chords represent the raising of the curtain and encapsulate the thrill of anticipation of the forth-coming events. The light, tripping violin passage sets the scene for magical goings-on. During the course of the overture, Mendelssohn manages to convey, alternately:

- The Athenian Court (grand theme, supported by trumpets)

- The 'rude mechanicals' (simple theme, accompanied by repeated chord on low strings)

- Bottom, braying with the asses head (direct mimicry, two notes slurred from high to low on upper strings)

- The enchanted wood (quiet high woodwind and brass, tremolando upper strings, pizzicato lower strings).

All this is achieved within the conventions of sonata form, which makes this an extremely accomplished work for a composer of any age, and a mark of genius in this case. Sixteen years later, Mendelssohn returned to this work and added several movements including the famous wedding march, and settings of Shakespeare's verses from the play, for a performance in Potsdam in 1843.

Inevitably, incidental music intended for the theatre finds its way into the concert hall, often at the instigation of the composer, who is more than happy to recycle existing works for further profitable exposure. The music takes on a separate existence as a concert item and becomes known as a standard part of the orchestral repertoire. For example Grieg's *Peer Gynt* suites 1 and 2, were rearrangements of music originally composed for the Ibsen lyrical drama in 1876. The themes from this have become divorced from their original dramatic meaning and are now enjoyed simply as music.

Film music

From the earliest days of cinema, music has played an integral part in the filmgoing experience. Early picture houses would employ a pianist to accompany silent movies with a repertoire of stock phrases to reflect the mood of the story pictured on the screen. The effectiveness of this system depended very much upon the skill and ingenuity of the pianist in linking the music to the action. Some of the larger cinemas added other instruments and sound effects to their musical arsenal, and professional musicians were employed. As more and more opulent picture palaces were created, the musical accompaniment became more ambitious, and some films were provided with full orchestral scores. Through the diligence and skill of musicians like Carl Davis, some of these scores have been reconstructed, and performances of epic silent films like *Ben Hur* are given with full orchestral accompaniment in concert halls, which can be adapted to accommodate both screen and orchestra.

With the advent of sound-recording techniques, music could be pre-recorded and synchronized with the screen action, and major studios in Hollywood employed hundreds of musicians and composers to provide the endless flow of music necessary to keep pace with the ever increasing output of the movie industry. Inevitably, much of this was derivative, vaguely reminiscent of composers who specialized in tone-painting, like Debussy, Delius, Wagner and Richard Strauss, plus the more 'modern' sounds of Stravinsky where the dramatic action demanded it. Some film composers were content merely to reflect the mood of a scene in a fairly unobtrusive way. Gradually, however, the creative possibilities of combining music and drama on film began to be explored. To pull out a single example, Max Steiner's score for *The Big Sleep*, has a suitably spiky Leitmotiv for Humphrey Bogart's portrayal of detective Philip Marlowe, which is transformed many times, following the hero's predicaments on screen.

Film makers also began to commission music from established composers, and there is a long list of distinguished names who have contributed to the genre, including Benjamin Britten, Erich Korngold, Arthur Honneger, William Walton, Arthur Bliss, Ralph Vaughan Williams, Aaron Copland, Leonard Bernstein and Sergei Prokofiev. Some music, originally composed for films, has been adapted for concert performance, such as Prokofiev's suite *Lieutenant Kijé* (1934), and his **cantata** *Alexander Nevsky* (1939), both of which began life as film music. Similarly, Vaughan Williams's seventh symphony, *Sinfonia Antartica* (1953), is a reworking of the music written for the film *Scott of the Antarctic*.

Above all, film music is eclectic. There are no boundaries, and film makers will cheerfully take extracts from all sorts of music if the director feels that the music provides the right ambience. The music of Strauss in *2001* was mentioned in Chapter 06, and the beautiful slow movement from Mozart's Piano Concerto No. 21 became the theme for *Elvira Madigan*. Of course, classical music is not the only source of film music. Jazz has been used most effectively, for example in Louis Malle's 1958 film *L'Ascenseur pour L'Echafaud* (Lift to the Scaffold) for which the music was improvised by trumpeter Miles Davis, with a small group of musicians. There have been film music scores drawn from just about every kind of music, from rock and pop to country and ethnic musics, but good film music does more than merely complement the visual image, it adds a new dimension to it. Who could forget the deep menacing two-note Leitmotiv of the shark in *Jaws*, or the screeching violin notes in the shower scene in *Psycho*? Not exactly memorable themes in their own right, but imagine those scenes without the music – the dramatic impact would be halved.

More recently, there have been interesting developments in the genre, for example, in Michael Nyman's music for Peter Greenaway's 1980s films. In *The Falls* and *Drowning by Numbers*, Nyman takes fragments of the slow movement of Mozart's *Sinfonia Concertante* for violin and viola, and subjects them to a number of variations. Concentrating on short phrases, Nyman explores every nuance of music, and the repetition of these phrases creates a hypnotic effect which adds to the power of Greenaway's screen images. Minimalist techniques like this are discussed in more detail in Chapter 14.

Music for television

All of the above remarks apply equally to television drama, but it's worth mentioning that there have been operatic works which were composed specifically for the medium of television. The first of these was *Amahl and the Night Visitors*, by Gian Carlo Menotti, which was televized in the United States in 1951. Since then there have been several others, the best-known and most successful in the United Kingdom being *Owen Wingrave* by Benjamin Britten (1913–77), which was based on a ghost story by Henry James and appeared on the small screen in 1971. Both of these works have since been adapted for production on stage, but the important thing is that composers have realised the potential of television as a medium for carrying opera to a wider audience, and have exploited its unique qualities, such as close-up shots, location work and effects that would be impossible to translate effectively to the stage.

the performance

In this chapter you will learn:

- that music comes to life only in performance, and in this chapter we arrive at that point, taking in the conductor, the orchestra and the soloist, in both live and recorded performances

- about that most familiar of instruments – the piano.

Music exists only in performance, and each performance is different. They are influenced by many different factors including players, conductors, venues and intangibles like the collective mood of the orchestra, the atmosphere in the auditorium, the attitude of the audience, and so on. It is a delicate line of communication that runs from the composer's mind, via the printed score, realized by musicians, and presented to the audience. These all-too-human variables ensure that no two performances are identical, but that's part of the beauty of it. Let's look at some of the different elements involved.

The conductor

One of the mysteries about the world of classical music to the casual observer is the fact that there is almost always a person on a raised podium, with his or her back to the audience gesticulating to the orchestra, who may, or may not seem to be taking much notice. What, we wonder, is their precise function in the making of music? All the instructions for dynamics and phrasing are given in the individual players' written parts, so surely it is only necessary to agree on the tempo and play the music as written? Why can't they play without a conductor?

Well, actually it has been tried in the former Soviet Union from 1922, when a conductorless orchestra (*persimfans*) was formed in Moscow. Briefly, this was an overzealous application of socialist principles, the autocratic position of the conductor, making musical decisions without due consultation with comrades, being unacceptable. The experiment was granted a government subsidy in 1925, and success was claimed, but each performance required many hours of rehearsal time for the players to agree on the details. It was also pointed out that the musicians involved were all seasoned players, having worked for many years with different conductors. With less experienced instrumentalists, the task would have been much more problematical. Other attempts were made in the 1920s to dispense with the conductor (experiments in Budapest and New York were reported), but none seems to have met with any prolonged success.

The conductor is inevitably something of an autocrat. Whatever he or she desires in the way of performance must be implemented, as nearly as possible, by the orchestral players. But how did this state of affairs come about? No one knows when the first person stood up and waved an arm to indicate that the music should begin, but we know that from about the fifteenth century it was the practice for the choral music of the time to be regulated by means of a short stick or a roll of paper, wielded by a leader or principal singer. Contemporary paintings and engravings reveal that, during the seventeenth and eighteenth centuries, performances were often directed from the keyboard (harpsichord or organ at first, later piano). The conductor would play occasionally to indicate important musical landmarks, changes of tempo and the like, and might also use a baton or rolled paper to beat time, sometimes quite audibly.

Conducting could also be a hazardous occupation. Jean-Baptiste Lully (see Chapter 07), composer to Louis XIV, was also a favourite of that corrupt monarch, and became rich and influential as a consequence. He was put in charge of the court orchestra, and it fell to him to conduct a Te Deum (hymn of praise) dedicated to the then ailing king. Lully affected a long baton or stave which he would thump on the floor to emphazise the tempo, and, during a particularly emphatic bout of time-keeping, he struck his foot, causing an injury which became infected and rapidly brought about his death. The king recovered and lived for another 28 years.

Haydn and Mozart would have conducted performances of their works from the keyboard, possibly in conjunction with the leader of the orchestra (principal of the first violins), who might direct the proceedings with a wave of his bow. In Haydn's London concerts (1791 and 1794), which were given in conjunction with the violinist and impresario Johann Salomon, the two directed the orchestra from the piano and first violin chairs. This practice has returned to some extent, particularly in the activities of pianist-conductors like Daniel Barenboim and Vladimir Ashkenazy, who play and conduct Mozart piano concertos from the keyboard with great success.

Gradually, the conductor moved away from the keyboard, and the baton was restored, albeit in a more refined form. During the course of the nineteenth century, it became normal practice for the orchestra to be directed by a non-playing conductor in the way that we would recognize today. There are tragic accounts of the deaf Beethoven conducting his own works with exaggerated gestures, crouching down to indicate a quiet passage, and rising to signal a crescendo, not always in time with the orchestra. These sad testimonies do, however, illustrate the changing function of the conductor, in that Beethoven was directing the dynamic

expression of the music rather than merely beating time.

Louis Spohr (1784–1859), famous in his time as a conductor, composer and violinist, introduced the baton to London in 1820, to the surprise of the concert organizers, who expected him to lead with the violin, and had provided a pianist to assist in directing the orchestra. Spohr dispensed with the assistant, and his violin remained in its case. Instead he produced a small ivory baton and astonished the London audience by controlling the proceedings with nothing more than this. Other composers followed suit when called upon to conduct their own works. Mendelssohn brought the baton to Leipzig in 1835, and Schumann to Dusseldorf in 1853, in both cases encountering local opposition. Weber and Spontini pioneered this form of conducting in the operatic field.

The precision of some early conductors evidently left something to be desired, however. In his *Memoirs*, Berlioz describes the first performance of his *Requiem*, conducted by François Habenek, an established and well-respected conductor who gave the first performances of Beethoven's symphonies in France. The *Requiem* is a tricky piece to conduct, requiring, in addition to a huge orchestra and choir, four brass ensembles to be placed one in each corner of the building. It is essential for the conductor to give clear indications of tempo, visible to all the separate groups of musicians and singers. Berlioz describes the crucial moment, just after the Dies Irae (Day of Wrath), when the tempo is halved and the brass groups begin a tumultuous fanfare:

Habenek laid down his baton and, calmly producing his snuff-box, proceeded to take a pinch of snuff. I had been keeping my eye on him. In a flash I turned on my heel, sprang forward in front of him and, stretching out my arm, marked out the four great beats of the new tempo. The bands followed me and everything went off in order. I conducted the piece to the end. The effect I had dreamed of was attained.

There was some controversy later about the veracity of Berlioz's account of this incident, and the motivation for Habenek's behaviour. It may have been a case of incompetence or malice. Berlioz had a number of enemies in Paris, and Habenek was associated with some of them. But the fact remains that the snuff-taking incident was by no means unusual or unbelievable in the Paris of 1825. Berlioz concludes:

Unhappy composers! Learn to conduct yourselves (in both senses of the word); for conductors, never forget, are the most dangerous of all your interpreters.

Berlioz was ahead of his time in many ways. He understood that it was necessary for the conductor to have a comprehensive knowledge and understanding of the music, and the ability to communicate that knowledge clearly and confidently to the musicians in his charge. It was not enough just to set the tempo and keep the orchestra together. With the power of leadership came the responsibility of producing an intelligent and sensitive interpretation of the music. There gradually grew up a new generation of conductors who took this responsibility seriously, like Hans von Bülow, Hans Richter, Richard Wagner and in England, Charles Hallé, who founded the Manchester orchestra bearing his name, which flourishes today.

The twentieth century saw the rise of the celebrity conductor. Members of this species were essentially specialists in the art of conducting, not normally composers or renowned instrumentalists. They were, and are, a product of their time; twentieth-century advances in communication, travel, broadcasting and recording made possible their worldwide recognition. Arturo Toscanini (1867–1957) was one of the most charismatic and, some would say, the greatest of this new breed. Like many of the conductors of his generation, he was a martinet, famous for his tantrums at rehearsals. However, he achieved some marvellous results, and even through the monophonic mists of time, his recordings have an unparalleled clarity and energy.

Not all conductors are as fiery and irascible as Toscanini, and that sort of behaviour would certainly not be tolerated by today's orchestral players. But the rehearsal is the crucial time when conductors must convey their ideas about the music to a group of people they may never have met before. The conductor must begin the rehearsal with a clear idea of how the music should be played, and must have the ability to realize this individual concept with musicians who may have played the same pieces with dozens of other conductors.

Technical matters of tempo, dynamics, phrasing and balance must be decided by the conductor, and individual views of these can vary considerably. But a wider vision of the work must also be demonstrated to produce a performance which will convince the audience of its intelligence, confidence and integrity. A successful performance should provide a well-rounded and satisfying musical experience for the listener, who is not concerned with the technical and interpretative problems faced by the performers.

So, when all the many difficulties have been overcome, there is still a magical ingredient which enables one conductor to draw a fine or even great performance from an orchestra, and another to produce a routine, lacklustre effort from the same musicians. Extravagant physical gestures are not the answer to this riddle: Adrian Boult's hand movements were minimal, but the musical results were exceptional. Toscanini was said to have burning eyes with which he would ignite the passions of the orchestra, but Herbert von Karajan often conducted with his eyes closed. Some, like von Karajan and Thomas Beecham would conduct from memory, while others would always have the score in front of them. There is no set pattern for success in the art of conducting.

We have to accept that there is an intangible element in the communication between conductor and orchestra. Those who can achieve great performances, which leave us thrilled and gratified, are genuinely gifted individuals. Perhaps this is why we allow them superstar status, and heap all kinds of honours on their heads. They can create something we value and enjoy, but cannot explain.

Recorded music

A recording, however painstakingly produced, captures only one performance (although one recorded performance can be a composite of several different 'takes'). You can listen to two or more recordings of the same piece by the same orchestra under the same conductor, and find them quite different in detail. Herbert von Karajan recorded the Beethoven symphonies three times in stereo, partly because he was interested in keeping up to date with advances in recording techniques (the last was a digital version), but also because he was constantly revising his view of the music. He once said to the young conductor Simon Rattle that after the first hundred performances of the Fifth Symphony, one begins to understand the work! Perhaps this constant mental activity contributes to the longevity of many conductors (von Karajan died in 1989, at the relatively early age of 81).

When choosing which version of a piece to buy, you should try to listen to as many different recordings as possible, and let your ear decide which one you prefer, rather than relying on famous names or record-company hype. Listening to the radio can help here. You could look through your listings magazine, and make a note of all the pieces you are interested in. In the United Kingdom, from time to time, BBC Radio 3 broadcasts programmes in which different recordings of a piece are compared and evaluated. These can be quite an ear-opener as the differences in interpretation and execution are highlighted. If you can tune into any of these or similar programmes you will find them fascinating, and helpful, when it comes to making your own choices.

The orchestra

The conductor may be a genius, with a special insight into the composer's mind, but the quality of the performance will depend upon the orchestra, the instrument through which the composer's ideas and the conductor's insight is translated from the dry printed page into sound. The orchestra ultimately makes the music. We have already looked at its four main component parts: strings, woodwind, brass and percussion, and we shall trace the evolution of this wonderful machine through musical history in Part Two.

The orchestra 'live'

At that most exciting of events, an orchestral concert, we begin to savour those delicious minutes of anticipation when the members of the orchestra file on to the platform with their instruments, take their places, and begin to tune up. The oboe gives out the note that all the other instruments tune to, and there follows a general fussing with technicalities – tightening or slackening strings, adjusting mouthpieces (woodwind), tuning slides (brass) and testing. The timpani need to be tuned too, and a dark tapping can be heard from the rear of the platform. This cacophony is the raw material from which the composer's edifice will be constructed. Once the orchestra is tuned and settled, the leader appears on the platform, and bows to the applause. When he or she is seated, the conductor enters, acknowledges the applause, and raises the baton to begin the piece.

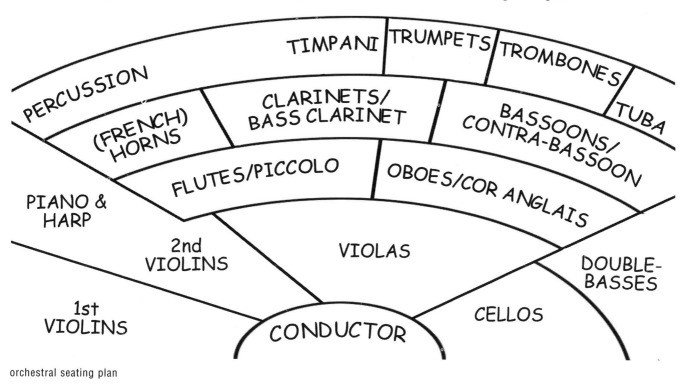

orchestral seating plan

The leader

The leader is in many ways comparable to the earlier violinist/director, and performances of Baroque music (see Chapter 10) are often directed by the leader, with no conductor present. In a modern orchestra, the leader is always the principal first violinist (called the Concertmaster in the United States), and the first violins match their bowing and phrasing to that of the leader to ensure a homogeneous sound from the most important section of the orchestra. The leader is always placed at the front of the platform, to the left of the conductor, with the rest of the first violins spread across the platform to the left.

Platform placings

Platform placings can vary, but a typical layout would comprise the second violins fanning out behind the firsts, to the left of the conductor, followed by the violas (in front of the conductor), cellos to the right, followed by double-basses. There may be some changes in detail, but you can always expect to see the strings spread across the front of the platform. String players are seated in pairs, sharing one music stand or 'desk'. Generally the woodwind come next, with the brass behind them, and the percussion at the rear with the timpani at the centre, level with the conductor.

The most significant deviation from this typical seating plan is historical. In the nineteenth and early twentieth centuries, it was common practice to place the second violins to the right of the conductor, so all the violins were at the front of the platform. All the great orchestral works of that period would probably have been performed in this format and those who wish to reconstruct the conditions of the original performances tend to lay out their violins in this way. Which brings us to the vexed question of authenticity.

The authenticity debate

Since the 1970s (it is difficult to date precisely), there has been an explosion of interest in 'authentic' performances. That means the attempt to reproduce as closely as possible the sounds and style of performance that the composer might have heard. Accurate replicas of instruments have been made, and musicians have adapted their techniques to become proficient at playing them. Gut strings are used in preference to the modern steel or wire-wound ones. Woodwind instruments without the benefit of modern keying systems have been reconstructed, and 'natural' horns and trumpets, without valves, built and mastered by a dedicated band of enthusiasts. This band has grown over the years, and both live and recorded performances on period instruments are now quite common.

Obviously this orchestra sounds different from its modern counterpart, but added to this is a scholarly effort to recreate the original performance practices. When we hear a performance by an 'authentic' music group, we might hear familiar music sounding slightly 'odd', with a different instrumental sound, and tempos we are not used to. The tendency over the years has been to adapt the music of earlier times to later styles. For example, generations of musicians looked at eighteenth-century music through eyes (and ears) conditioned by their nineteenth- and twentieth-century experience. They gradually altered the balance of the orchestra and changed the style of playing to produce a smooth, romantic gloss, which was never part of the original conception of the music. The 'authentic' movement is an attempt to rectify this. Clearly, there is a debate about the quest for authenticity. A brief summary of the two viewpoints might be:

For

It is the duty of the performer to be aware of the historical conditions under which the piece was composed and performed, and to recreate as faithfully as possible those conditions and performance practices. By so doing we may discover the true character of the music as the composer intended it.

Against

We can never know for certain how a piece was originally played. Any attempt at authentic performance involves a certain amount of guesswork, however educated. We can't discount our listening experience and hear a piece with eighteenth-century ears, so we can never replicate the contemporary aural experience. In any case, why should we not bring new ideas about interpretation to the performance?

What you, the listener, must do is audition the two types of performance and decide which you prefer. As both approaches have their merits, it is not impossible to enjoy both equally. You can't hear too many different versions of a piece of music. Each orchestra and conductor, whether dedicated to 'authenticity' or not, has something different to offer in interpretation (and reinterpretation).

The soloist

In our concert, the other person who may emerge from the wings after the leader and the conductor is the soloist. Concertos are popular constituents of concert programmes, and there is an international coterie of 'star' soloists whose names will ensure ticket sales wherever they appear. In a concerto, the autocratic regime of the conductor is sidelined as it is the soloist who should make the major decisions of tempo, phrasing, dynamics and other factors which contribute to the individual performance. It was around the turn of the nineteenth century when the phenomenon of the itinerant virtuoso performer first appeared, and this largely followed the growth in popularity of the piano. Invented at the beginning of the eighteenth century, the fortepiano, as it was originally called, superceded instruments like the harpsichord and the spinet, gradually becoming popular for home music making, and eventually for solo concert performances.

The purchasers of pianos were generally members of the burgeoning middle classes (the novels of Jane Austen are full of references to home performers of varying ability), whose musical tastes were not always of the most serious and high-minded nature. The same part of the population formed the bulk of the audiences at public concerts, and to ensure a capacity attendance, the virtuosos chose pieces with maximum technical effect and often minimal musical content. Variations on popular themes were favourites, and these would include pianistic devices like fast runs, octaves in both hands and **arpeggios** (spread chords), calculated to impress the audience with the

---

The pianoforte

Very simply, the strings inside the piano are stretched across a frame and struck with felt hammers, mechanically connected to the keys, the vibration of the string being stopped by a system of felt dampers. The instrument was invented by Bartolommeo Christofori at the beginning of the eighteenth century, and provided much more scope for variation in dynamics than its predecessors, hence its name (literally 'soft–loud'). Some early examples were described as 'fortepianos', and this name is now applied to replicas of those instruments, used in performance today. The iron frame (patented in 1820) brought extra volume and carrying power, enabling a performer to be heard in a concert hall full of paying customers.

[Earlier keyboard instruments are described in Chapter 09.]

---

player's skill. Even Liszt, the greatest virtuoso of his time, composed and played some pieces of this type. He was accorded what amounted to an early version of the 'star status' familiar today, and greeted by adoring crowds wherever he went. His concerts were always sold out and made large amounts of money, enabling him to live and compose in a style that befitted his talents.

The virtuoso violinist and composer Nicolo Paganini (1782–1840) would intersperse his concertos and caprices (fine compositions which are played today) with stage business like playing blindfolded, mimicking birdsong, and similar stunts. He was tall, gaunt and dark, and his compositions were considered to be so difficult as to be impossible to play without some kind of magical assistance. The story spread that he was in league with the devil, a good example of early PR hype which was extremely effective. Berlioz was commissioned by Paganini to write a showpiece for viola and orchestra, as the virtuoso wanted to exhibit his prowess on that instrument as well as the violin. The result was *Harold in Italy*, which is more properly described as a symphony with viola **obbligato** than a viola concerto. The piece is loosely based on Byron's *Childe Harold's Pilgrimage*, with the viola representing the poetic hero. Unfortunately, Paganini was not happy with the piece, because the solo part was not spectacular or prominent enough, 'I must be playing all the time,' he told the composer.

Nowadays, soloists are not expected to indulge in crowd-pleasing stunts (except for recitals by groups of operatic tenors!), but there is a constant demand for the popular concertos, which soloists sometimes complain are restricting in creative terms. One solution is to commission new pieces from contemporary composers, expanding the repertoire with an influx of fresh material. Another is to revive neglected works from earlier periods which may have become the victims of changes in fashion and are ripe for re-evaluation. The violinist Fritz Kreisler (1875–1962) went further than this, composing pieces in an antique style and presenting them as newly discovered masterpieces by obscure composers.

Solo and chamber music

When developing your listening habits, don't forget the solo repertoire. Like orchestras, soloists have their own individual musical fingerprints, and you can audition them to discover all the individual nuances of their playing. Much of the greatest music was written for a single instrument, and it's worth investigating particularly keyboard pieces from composers of all ages.

Chamber music is another hugely important area. Many composers chose the intimacy of chamber forms, particularly the **string quartet**, to express their profoundest musical thoughts. We'll look a little more closely at the origins and history of chamber music in Part Two, but in the meantime, why not treat yourself to a musical interlude?

I hope that, when you listen to your chosen piece, you think about the various aspects of listening to music that we have covered in Part One of this book. Here is a brief summary of the main points:

● **Listening below the surface**

Think about melody and accompaniment. Identify the roles of the different instruments.

● **Elements of music: melody, harmony and rhythm**

How do they contribute to the character of the piece?

● **Type of work: symphony, concerto, etc.**

What do you expect to hear, orchestra, solo instruments, voices?

● **Form**

How is the piece constructed? Follow the composer's discussion of the musical ideas.

● **Pictures and stories**

Is there an outside influence you should know about? If so, does it help you to understand the piece? Decide whether you want to follow it or not.

● **Performance**

It's your choice here – select a conductor and an orchestra, and, if relevant, a soloist whose work you like, sit back and enjoy the music.

summary of listening points

part

two

era and style

introduction

Music, like any other art, is a product of its era, and we can better understand and appreciate it if we are aware of the historical conditions at the time of its conception. In Part One we exercised our ears and studied the structure and rationale behind different types of music, now we must put all this into an historical context, because:

- Music from a given period has certain stylistic characteristics which are recognizable and identifiable, and which transcend differences between individual composers. For example, Bach and Handel wrote very different music for most of their parallel lives (they were almost exact contemporaries), but their music is linked by the stylistic conventions and compositional practices of the period, which we shall look at in Chapter 10. As we saw in Part One, forms change radically through the passage of time, for example a concerto in Bach's time was very different from a nineteenth-century Romantic concerto.

- The sound of the orchestra alters and develops with the different periods. We'll be looking at the development of the orchestra as we go along.

- If you know something of a composer's historical background, you will have some idea of what to expect from the above elements of composition and orchestra. You can acquire a sympathy for a style, and then extend your experience of that style by experimenting with other composers of the same period.

- Knowledge of the prevailing circumstances and constraints under which a composer was employed can provide clues about the type of pieces written. One of the duties of the cantor of Leipzig, for example, was to compose and perform a new cantata every week, hence we have more than 200 examples of the form from Bach. There are a similar number of concertos from the pen of Vivaldi, for similar contractual reasons in Venice. Haydn produced a large number of baryton trios, for the simple reason that his employer, Prince Esterházy, was an enthusiastic player of that (now obsolete) stringed instrument.

Historical conditions are a fundamental part of the music. They mould the style, dictate the form and prescribe the very nature of the sounds that the composers conceive. Let's now look at the historical framework of Western classical music.

09 early music – to the seventeenth century

In this chapter you will learn:

- about the history of music from plainsong to the sophistications of the early Baroque composers across Europe

- about some early instruments and the forms of music associated with them

- about the rise of opera and oratorio during this period.

As there is a limited amount of space available, and any account of music history must be somewhat selective, this section spans a relatively large chunk of time. We came briefly across Gregorian chant in Chapter 02 in the context of melody, and indeed the absence of harmony makes this a very pure form of melody. Plainsong, of which Gregorian chant became the dominant variety, began in the early centuries of Christianity, but its roots were in the Jewish synagogue and the Greek system of **modes** (forms of scales). Gradually, other voices were added in harmony to the chant, and the rhythms became regularized, rather than purely dictated by the text. Only around the thirteenth century did the term 'plainsong' come into being, to differentiate between the plain, undecorated chant, and the 'measured song' of the newer practices.

In the fourteenth and fifteenth centuries, **polyphonic** (literally 'many voiced') writing was developed. Different melodic lines began to move independently, common devices being imitation: one voice following another with the same, or similar tune, and **canon**, which is a stricter form of imitation, with voices following one another at a fixed distance. We've all tried our hands at simple canons like 'Row, Row, Row your boat', or 'London's Burning', and they can be great fun. A medieval English one is 'Sumer is icumen in', which is often performed by early music groups to great effect, sometimes with audience participation. Some early polyphonists were: John Dunstable (1370–1453), Guillaume Dufay (c.1400–74) and Josquin des Prés (c.1440–1521). These composers wrote only vocal music, the bulk of which was religious, with the addition of some secular songs. Josquin in particular was a master of the techniques of polyphonic part-writing, producing more than 30 Masses, 50 **motets** and 70 songs.

The sixteenth century saw further progress in vocal polyphony across Europe, with Palestrina (1525–94) in Italy, Victoria (1548–1611) in Spain, Lassus (1532–94) of the Flemish school and the Englishman William Byrd (1543–1623), about whom more later. About this time, composers began to take an interest in writing for instruments, and these could be divided into two main types: indoor and outdoor. The indoor instruments, designed for domestic use, included the lute, recorder, viols and keyboard instruments such as the virginals, spinet and harpsichord.

The lute

A stringed instrument, not unlike the guitar, except that the body is shaped like a half a pear, cut longways from top to bottom. A fingerboard extends from the narrow end of the body and strings are stretched over the instrument and plucked by the player. The number of strings was normally 11, five pairs and a single top string.

Viols

These are bowed stringed instruments, similar in appearance to the violin family, except that the back was generally flat and the fingerboard 'fretted' across with gut or metal, like that of a guitar. Viols were played in an upright position, rather than under the chin, and were commonly found in three sizes: treble or descant, tenor and bass (or *viola da gamba*, literally 'leg viol' (because it was placed between the legs, like the cello)). A set of these instruments for domestic use was known as a 'chest of viols', after the purpose-built piece of furniture in which they were stored. A typical ensemble, or 'consort' of viols might comprise pairs of each size of instrument with the possible addition of an alto and a double-bass viol (also called violone).

Harpsichord family

Inside the body of these keyboard instruments, the strings are plucked with small quills or tongues, fixed to upright posts, which are attached to the extremities of the keys (see Chapter 08 for comparison with the piano). Earlier forms had a single keyboard

viola d'amore (tenor viol)   *viola da gamba*

and set of strings (virginals and spinet), but later developments included double and even triple keyboards, and devices to give a variety of effects and variations in tone and volume.

Recorder

The recorder, or end-blown flute, has already been mentioned in Chapter 03. In the sixteenth century, a consort of recorders would normally consist of (from the highest to the lowest): descant, treble, tenor and bass. While the higher instruments were quite satisfactory, the lower were (and are) weaker in sound and more difficult to control.

Instrumental music

The music written for instruments fell into one of the following forms: adaptations of vocal polyphonic pieces, theme and variations, fantasias (or fancies) and dance music. To these may be added the accompaniment of songs, in which the lute was the most important instrument. John Dowland (1563–1626) excelled in this form of composition, and his four books of 'ayres' are available in modern editions for specialist performers today. Undoubtedly the finest keyboard music of this time was composed in England by three notable composers: William Byrd (1543–1623), John Bull (1563–1628) and Orlando Gibbons (1583–1625). In 1611 *Parthenia*, a book of pieces for the virginals, was published, subtitled *The Maydenhead of the first musicke that ever was printed for the Virginalls*. This contained the work of Byrd, Bull and Gibbons, and was in fact the first music to be printed from engraved plates in Britain. The music consists mainly of pieces in two dance forms, the slow **pavane** and the more lively **galliard**.

On the title page of the *Parthenia* is an engraving of a young woman at the keyboard, and she represents the intended user of the collection. It was considered an essential part of the young lady's accomplishments to be able to play the virginals (hence the name of the instrument). In fact, on many instruments the colouring of the keys was reversed so that the black keys would display the player's elegant white fingers to advantage as they moved gracefully across the keyboard. Other collection of pieces for the virginals were published in the wake of the *Parthenia*, and these form a valuable record from the period that has been called the 'golden age' of English music.

Early composers of instrumental music did not always specify the instruments on which it was to be performed, so it would be quite possible to have the same piece played in the home on a consort of viols, and to be given an outdoor performance on more strident instruments like the shawm, crumhorn, cornett and sackbut.

Early forms

A popular type of composition at this time was the **canzona**, which means 'song', but was also applied to instrumental works based on vocal forms. The **ricercare** ('seeking out'), was a free interpretation of one or more themes and is indistinguishable from the fantasia, mentioned earlier in this chapter. These forms were often used by the organist-composers, who also made a significant contribution to the growth of instrumental music in the sixteenth and seventeenth centuries (see 'Music for the organ', on page 57). Organ music became more adventurous with musicians like Claudio Merulo (1533–1604) of Venice, who would introduce **toccatas** (literally 'touch') of a showy nature as well as the more workmanlike and serious ricercares.

The final type of instrumental composition to be considered briefly, is the representational or programme piece, which was mentioned in Chapter 05, in connection with the French composer Clement Janequin (1474–1560). He specialized in pictorial *chansons* (like canzonas), vocal depictions of birdsong, hunting scenes and battles. William Byrd indulged in one battle piece for virginals, although it cannot be considered one of his greatest works. But this was a time of experimentation, change and development.

The growth of opera

Italy

Around the turn of the seventeenth century, a group of intellectuals, musicians, singers and poets met at the house of Count Giovanni Bardi (1534–1612) in Florence, to air their grievances about the shortcomings of the polyphonic style. They considered that the clarity and beauty of the poetry was fragmented by the overlaying of the different melodic lines that is the essence of polyphony. Their remedy was a return to the ideals of ancient Greek drama as they saw them, with the words

Shawms and crumhorns

These double-reed woodwind instruments were the forerunners of the modern oboe family (oboe, cor anglais and bassoon). They were made in various sizes, and the shawm was generally straight, while the crumhorn was curved at the end, rather like a walking stick. Both instruments had a series of finger holes, and perhaps one or two keys at the lower end of the instrument. In larger shawms the reed was fitted to a tube protruding from the body of the instrument in a way similar to the bassoon. In some crumhorns, the double reed was enclosed in a cap which protected the reed, but gave the player less control over the sound produced. These instruments produced a fairly coarse sound with little scope for variation in dynamics, but would have been useful in performing music in the open air, or for large groups of people.

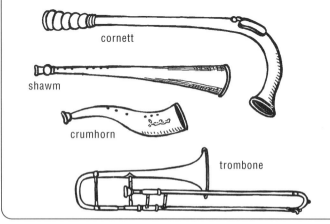

cornett

shawm

crumhorn

trombone

The cornett

Not to be confused with the cornet (see Chapter 06), this instrument was made of wood, or sometimes ivory, rather than brass, and is curved like an animal horn, with finger holes drilled along its length. The mouthpiece, sometimes attached to the instrument, but occasionally carved into it, is similar to that of a trumpet. It is cup-shaped, and the sound is produced by the vibration of the player's lips. The cornett is capable of a wide range of dynamic variation, from a soft, mellow sound to an incisive forte, and, in the hands of a skilful player, can execute rapid passages with great fluency.

The sackbut

This instrument is identical in method of construction and playing technique to the modern trombone. However, the bore of the tubing is narrower and the bell smaller, so the tone is lighter and quieter, making it an ideal partner for the cornett. The two were often combined in ensembles for church and ceremonial purposes, and were employed on the most important occasions as 'Music for His Majesty's Sackbuts and Cornetts', by Matthew Locke, the Master of the King's Music, for the coronation of Charles II, in 1660.

being declaimed musically, but with the music following the natural speech patterns in a single melody. This became formalized as **recitative**, the basis of the first operas which were composed by Jacopo Peri (1561–1633), and staged at the palace of Count Jacopo Corsi, both of whom were members of this new circle known as the *camerata*. The music for the first opera, *La Dafne*, performed in 1597, has been lost, but the next, *Euridice* (1600), has survived.

If you know what a recitative sounds like, even in a Mozart opera, you can imagine that a whole opera composed of nothing but recitative would be pretty dull. Fortunately, there was a genius waiting in the wings. Claudio Monteverdi (1567–1643) began in the service of the Duke of Mantua in the 1590s as a violinist, becoming *maestro di capella* (music master) around 1602. He moved to St Marks, Venice, in 1613, and was ordained a priest in 1632.

In addition to religious music Monteverdi became interested in opera, and his earliest work in this form, *Orfeo* (1603), followed Peri's *Euridice* in concept and subject matter. Monteverdi's *Orfeo* was notable for its adventurous use of the orchestra as well as **madrigal**-style vocal pieces breaking up the recitatives. Gradually, songs and duets became an integral part of the opera, and the **recitative** was relegated to a linking role between them, as well as a method of moving on the narrative. Monteverdi's last opera *The Coronation of Poppea* (1642) is constructed in this way. The Neapolitan composer Alessandro Scarlatti (c.1660–1725) refined the Italian style in the second half of the seventeenth century. He introduced the **da capo** aria, in ternary form (A–B–A), with the repeat of the 'A' section, embellished by the singer. The Italian overture, in three sections, fast–slow–fast (discussed in Chapter 04), was also a feature of Scarlatti's later operas.

France and England

Most of Europe adopted the fashionable Italian operatic style, but the French preferred their home-grown product. We have already met Jean-Baptiste Lully (or Lulli – ironically, he was of Italian descent) in Chapter 07 and we have seen that French operas did not follow the Italian pattern, for example in the invariable inclusion of ballet numbers. The chorus was also featured to a greater extent in French opera. In England opera was slow to develop, the prevailing form of musical entertainment in

the seventeenth century was the masque (briefly mentioned in Chapter 07), which combined music, drama, dance and pageantry, mainly for an aristocratic audience, who would often take an active part in the proceedings. Early English opera is dominated by a single enormously significant work, *Dido and Aeneas*, by Henry Purcell (1659–95). This is a true opera, with an overture in the French style, recitatives and arias. It was originally written for performance by the pupils of a girls' boarding school, and runs for about an hour.

Particularly memorable is the intensely moving final lament by Dido, 'When I am laid in earth', in which the tragedy of the abandoned lover is intensified by Purcell's poignant melody. At the root of the accompaniment is a ground bass, which is a series of notes (in this case 11) repeated to create a dirge-like effect over which Dido sings her heartbreaking aria. The vocal line and the ground bass do not begin and end together, they overlap to give a feeling of forward momentum to the piece, as Dido moves inexorably towards the grave she seeks. Having practised listening below the surface, you will be able to appreciate the genius of this construction to the full.

Oratorio

Religious vocal music progressed rather more slowly than opera, but change was inevitable, as the older style of polyphony, based on Greek modes began to die out. The religious equivalent of the opera was **oratorio**, which featured recitatives and arias in the operatic manner. The form originated in the sixteenth century, in the oratory of St Philip Neri in Rome, hence the name. The earliest known example is Emilio de Cavalieri's *Rappresentazione di Anima e di Corpo* (Representation of the Soul and the Body), which was first performed in 1600. Oratorio reached creative peaks in the works of Handel (*Messiah* is the best known example, although he wrote many others, see page 62), the *Passions* of J. S. Bach (page 61), and Haydn's *The Creation* (page 66).

The instrumental canzona and the early sonata

In Italy, vocal canzonas were often transcribed for instrumental performance, with no modification of the melodic lines. This canzona sonata evolved into a more characteristically instrumental style, with several contrasting sections, including movements in dance-forms. The early sonata was very different from the later model, which was outlined in Chapter 03. In the seventeenth century, a sonata was simply a work that was played (remember *sonare* = sound), as opposed to a cantata, which was sung. Sonatas tended to be written for small numbers of instruments, often strings or keyboards, and were divided into two types: *sonata da chiesa* and *sonata da camera* (church and chamber sonatas). At the same time the viols were becoming supplanted by the newer instruments of the violin family.

Indeed, from the late sixteenth to early eighteenth centuries the finest violins were made. Cremona, in Italy, was the birthplace of several families of violin makers whose work has never been surpassed. Nicolo Amati, was of the third generation of these craftsmen, but his pupil Antonio Stradivari (1644–1737) became the best-known and probably the greatest of them all. Giuseppe Guarneri (1687–1744) carried on the tradition with equal skill, and the instruments of all these makers are highly prized and treasured by violinists to the present day.

The expressive qualities of the violins were superior to those of the viols, being capable of greater dynamic range, brilliancy of tone and facility of fingering (having four strings rather than six and a curved fingerboard). The violin therefore lent itself more readily to solo playing, and has retained its pre-eminent position in all types of ensemble since its introduction in the seventeenth century. In the second half of the century, a great many sonatas were written for one or two violins, or a trio of two violins and cello. However, the description of these pieces can be a little confusing. A trio sonata, for example, would normally involve not three, but four musicians: two violinists, a cellist and keyboard player. The reason for this apparent anomaly is that there was an assumption that an instrumental accompaniment would be provided, so there was no necessity to advertise its presence.

The continuo

A specific form of accompaniment appeared when the old choral type of polyphonic writing, involving the weaving together of different strands of melody, was displaced by the recitative, which was accompanied by chordal harmony. A line of music was written beneath the melodic parts, and this was the foundation on which the accompaniment was to be built. Figures beneath the line indicated the harmony to be used, so a chord-playing instrument such as the harpsichord, organ or lute was necessary to fill in the accompaniment according to the instructions. Known variously as 'figured bass', 'thorough bass' or **basso continuo**, and eventually shortened to simply **continuo**, this method continued until the middle of the eighteenth century. So the trio sonata described above would comprise two violins, cello and continuo. Sometimes, another instrument would be added to strengthen or 'double' the bass line, giving extra weight to the ensemble. A solo sonata might therefore include three players: violin, plus a continuo of harpsichord and cello (or possibly viola da gamba, which remained in use as a continuo instrument).

Instrumental music in France

Around the middle in the seventeenth century there grew up a school of harpsichordists who specialized in suites of dances, reflecting the French taste, which emanated from the court. The most notable of these is Louis Marchand (1669–1732) and members of the Couperin family, of whom François (Couperin *le grand*, 1668–1733) expanded the form to include short mood pieces, or portraits, with titles like 'Regrets', 'Tender Languors' and 'The Enchantress'. It may surprise you to hear that our friend Lully was not involved in these keyboard works. Being a violinist, his contribution to French instrumental music was the creation of The King's Twenty-four Violins, which referred not only to violins, but members of the violin family, in this case violins, violas and cellos.

The dance suite

The **suite** in the seventeenth century might include a large number of different dances, but some occur more frequently than others. We touched on the pairing of the pavane and galliard earlier in this chapter in connection with Lully, but, by the second half of the century they had become unfashionable. After that time, the dances would invariably include the following:

Allemande
A fairly slow dance in duple time (two beats to the bar), which originated in Germany (hence the name, **allemande** meaning 'German').

Courante
Literally 'running', this moderately quick dance comes in two varieties. The Italian (*coranto* or *corrente*) version is a straightforward triple, but the French **courante** has a tendency to ambiguity, alternating between three and two beats to the bar.

Sarabande
A stately dance in moderately slow, triple time, with the second beat of the bar emphasized. Its origins are thought to be oriental and Spanish, and it was once considered to be dangerously erotic, rather like the tango in the early decades of the twentieth century.

Gigue
This lively dance has its roots in the jigs of England, Ireland and Scotland. The number of beats to the bar is variable, but listen for groups of three notes per beat. The **gigue** is often the closing movement of the suite.

These four dances, all in binary form (two sections, A–B, see Chapter 03) comprise the basic suite. They would normally be preceded by a prelude, which generally does not have such a strong rhythmic character and definite form as the movements that follow it, but is often more melodically adventurous. The trio *sonatas da camera* of Archangelo Corelli (1653–1713), for example, generally have a short, slow prelude in a free style, followed by *allemande*, *corrente*, *sarabanda* and *giga* or *gavotta*. Other dances would often appear, particularly in the French suites, and the most common of these was the minuet.

The minuet
A truly French dance, and the most important in terms of historical influence, the minuet began as a rustic folk-dance, and was introduced to the French court about 1650 by (you've guessed it) Lully, after which it began to make regular appearances in dance suites. As we saw in Chapter 04, the minuet (and trio) survived as part of the symphony until the end of the eighteenth century.

Music for the organ
Much important music was written for the organ in the seventeenth century, the work of organist-composers across Europe. Girolamo Frescobaldi (1583–1643), organist of St Peter's, Rome, expanded the repertoire that had been established by Merulo and his contemporaries in Venice. A parallel school of organ playing was founded in Amsterdam by Jan Pieterszoon Sweelinck (1562–1621). He had studied in Venice and passed on the style, with his own modifications and developments (he greatly admired the English virginalists, for example), to his pupils, many of whom were German.

Through the influence of Frescobaldi and Sweelinck and their pupils, an important tradition of organ playing grew up in Germany. The hymn-tunes or 'chorales' of the Lutheran Church were taken by these German organists as subjects for musical development. 'Chorale preludes', as they are generically called, fall into three main types: fantasy (or **fantasia**), a free interpretation, which could be improvised; **partita**, meaning variations (but beware, later composers, including Bach, used the word as synonymous with 'suite'); and finally fugue.

Fugue
The word itself has a fustian quality, suggesting to some a dry, impenetrable complexity, and to others a funereal dirge. Actually, the fugue is very different from those impressions. It is not as complicated as the name may suggest, and can be fast, flowing and exciting. The word is derived from the Latin *fuga*, meaning 'flight' (in the sense of running away), and the chief characteristic of fugue is imitation, with two or more melodic lines pursuing one another. The theme, or 'subject' can appear in the upper, lower or middle parts, and the 'answer' may be slightly altered or at a lower or higher pitch according to the harmonic framework of the piece.

This interweaving of separate strands of melody is called **counterpoint,** and is an essential element of fugue. The early German organists became adept at creating rich **contrapuntal** textures, using chorale tunes as their subjects. Johann Pachelbel (1653–1706) and Dietrich Buxtehude (1637–1707) were two of the early masters of the chorale prelude, but the form achieved its greatest height of creativity in the hands of Johann Sebastian Bach, as we shall see in Chapter 10.

late baroque

In this chapter you will learn:

- about the work of three great composers: Vivaldi, and the twin giants of the era, Bach and Handel

- the definitions of some musical terms

- about an important instrumental form used by all three of the above composers – the concerto grosso.

A quick word about definitions to begin with. You will almost certainly come across the term 'Baroque' when reading about music, choosing CDs or listening to broadcasts. The word in its current meaning is borrowed from architecture where it is used to describe the ornate designs of the seventeenth and eighteenth centuries. In musical terms, the Baroque era covers roughly the period from the beginning of the seventeenth century to the middle of the eighteenth, characterized by contrapuntal styles of writing. The period is sometimes broken up into early, middle and late, with the late or 'high' Baroque beginning around 1700.

If the seventeenth century was a time of great change and development, the eighteenth saw the fruition of great genius and the consolidation of musical forms and systems. The modal system had died out and been replaced by the major and minor scales and hence keys

(24 altogether, 12 major and 12 minor) that were used exclusively for the next 200 years and are still employed by composers today. The possibility of moving from one key to another during the course of a piece was one which composers eagerly grasped. By the beginning of the century this new system was more or less established, and an excellent vehicle for instrumental explorations was found in the concerto. The meaning of the word in the late seventeenth century was quite vague, signifying only a bringing together of musical forces, although there was always an implied element of contest or at least contrast. By the early 1700s a common form was the *concerto grosso*, having been pioneered by Italian composers like Corelli and Torelli of the Bolognese school.

The *concerto grosso*

The essence of this type of work is that two contrasting instrumental groups are pitted against each other. These are a solo group called the *concertino* or *concertante*, and the orchestral body (strings and continuo), which is the *ripieno*. The two groups play separately and together and there is a great deal of contrapuntal interplay. The usual structure was of three movements, fast–slow–fast, with a forceful driving momentum in the fast movements which became characteristic of the style. Corelli's concerti grossi were in many ways extensions of his trio sonatas, the concertino were often a trio of two violins and cello, with the ripieno strings added to the continuo. Some followed the movements of the dance suite as associated with the sonatas da camera as described in Chapter 09. Like the early sonatas, the concerto was often divided into two types: *concerto da chiesa* and *concerto da camera*.

The music of the eighteenth century was dominated by a handful of great names, so this chapter and the next will inevitably be focussed on the lives and works of these composers. Vivaldi occupies a crucial position in the transition to the late Baroque period, which was the domain of two musical giants, Bach and Handel.

Vivaldi

The concerto was further developed by Antonio Vivaldi (1676–1741), of Venice, who brought several innovations to the form. An accomplished violinist, like many Italian composers from the home of the violin, he introduced greater virtuosity into the solo violin parts, he also extended the scope of the solo instruments. He wrote concertos for single or pairs of solo instruments, including violins, oboes, flutes, trumpets and even mandolins, although some require no soloist at all. The most important qualities of Vivaldi's music are immediately felt: the simple but engaging themes, the infectious ebullience of the quick movements and the contrasts of mood in the more reflective moments. Unlike most of the composers discussed in Chapter 9, Vivaldi is a household name today, mainly due to the seemingly limitless appeal of *The Four Seasons*, for solo violin and string orchestra, which comprises four of a series of twelve concertos, subtitled 'the contest between harmony and invention'.

The Four Seasons

An early example of programme music, these concertos feature a host of descriptive writing, with birdsong, rain, thunder and even a barking dog in the second movement. Almost every bar can be related to an extra-musical picture, and lengthy summaries have been published. Nevertheless, this is music which has found favour with a mass audience 200 years after it was written. Sadly, Vivaldi died in poverty, and his music was ignored until its twentieth-century revival. Today, *The Four Seasons* is one of the most popular pieces of classical music, with a multitude of recorded versions available, and many performances offered each year; it also regails us in shops, hotel foyers and television advertisements. It's difficult to say exactly why this should be, but the great

jazz composer, bandleader and pianist Duke Ellington once said in music 'It don't mean a thing if it ain't got that swing' and this can be applied to the music of Vivaldi. When played well, it has a tremendous, unstoppable drive which is sure to quicken the pulse, and start the feet tapping.

Venice and travel

Vivaldi was the son of a violinist in the service of the Doge, and studied for the priesthood as well as music, becoming ordained in 1703. In his home town of Venice he became known as 'the red priest', because of the colouring of his hair. He never practised his vocation, pleading a respiratory problem, but was extremely busy as director of music of a girls' academy. He was granted a lot of time to travel abroad performing his music, particularly his operas (38 in all), and this sense of the theatrical probably contributed to the expressive effects in *The Four Seasons*. Despite his dispensation for travelling, he was still required to write two concertos a month for Venice, and the total of these is more than 400. In the solo concertos there is an almost operatic interplay between soloist and orchestra which looks ahead to the more dramatic elements of the virtuoso works of later centuries.

J. S. Bach

A great admirer of Vivaldi's music was the young Johann Sebastian Bach (1685–1750), who transcribed some of the violin concertos for harpsichord. Bach was born into a musical family, his father was a violinist and court trumpeter at Eisenach, Thuringia (now central Germany), and there seems to have been no doubt that Johann Sebastian would follow the same profession. It is a fact that Bach's professional appointments dictated to a great extent the nature of the compositions he produced. After studying the organ and the violin, he became a choral scholar at Lüneburg from whence he walked the 30 miles to Hamburg to hear the organist Johann Reinken, an exponent of the North German tradition, influenced by Sweelinck. In 1703 he took up a post as a violinist in the court orchestra of Prince Johann Ernst in Weimar, but this was to be a brief experience. Later the same year he moved to Arnstadt, first as violinist then organist in the new church, which is now called the Bachkirche in the composer's honour. During the four years spent at Arnstadt, Bach visited Lübeck to hear

Bach

form used by Buxtehude, and expands it enormously, with 20 variations on the theme preceding the mighty fugue.

Cöthen (1717–23)

When the Kapellmeister at Weimar died, Bach was not offered the position, and he resigned, obtaining instead the post of Kapellmeister to Prince Leopold of Anhalt-Cöthen. Again, historical circumstances shaped the musical output. As there was no music to be written in this Calvinist chapel, and consequently no substantial organ available, Bach turned out secular music for orchestra and harpsichord, all of which was greatly appreciated by Prince Leopold, who was a sincere admirer of the talents of his Kapellmeister. This happy time produced such masterworks as the French and English suites for harpsichord, the first book of the 'forty-eight' preludes and fugues entitled 'The Well-Tempered Clavier', and the Brandenburg Concertos.

The suites were both in the French style, but the English were larger in scope, beginning with preludes and including a greater variety of dances. The title 'English' was acquired when a manuscript copy was found with the words *fait pour les Anglais* (made for the English) written upon it. The 'forty-eight' refers to the first of two sets of 24 preludes and fugues, one in each of the major and minor keys. The 'well-tempered clavier' in the title simply prescribes an instrument ('clavier' is a general term for keyboard instruments) which is tuned in 'equal temperament', with 12 equally spaced notes to the octave, enabling the player to play equally tunefully in every key. These pieces had the effect of ending a debate about tuning. Some players had been advocating a system of accoustically accurate tuning which restricted the instrument to a few related keys, the more remote keys being excruciatingly out of tune.

The Brandenburg Concertos

The set of six concertos dedicated in 1721 to the Margrave of Brandenburg are well known and frequently performed today. They are excellent examples of the late Baroque concerto, three of which (nos. 2, 4 and 5) are true concerti grossi with groups of concertino solo instruments and ripieno strings. Of the others, numbers 3 and 6 are for contrasting groups of strings interacting contrapuntally. The first concerto is a little different, scored for pairs of oboes and horns, plus violino picolo

Buxtehude, further broadening his experience of German organ music.

Weimar (1708–17)

After a year as church organist at Mülhausen, Bach began his first major appointment. He became court organist to Duke Wilhelm Ernst at Weimar in 1708, at a good salary (which must have been most acceptable to the recently married young man), and prospects of promotion. After six years, he was indeed promoted to Konzertmeister, assistant to the ageing Kapellmeister, one of his duties in this new post being to write a cantata every month. The cantata at this time was like a mini-oratorio, for solo voices, chorus and orchestra, built around a chorale theme, and Bach's Weimar cantatas are works of great charm and originality. One familiar and beautiful example is 'Jesu, Joy of Man's Desiring'. But the most notable works from this period are the monumental organ pieces; fugues preceded by a toccata, prelude or **passacaglia** (a slow dance-form in triple time, similar to the **chaconne**). In these, the German organ tradition is carried forward to new heights of invention. The Passacaglia and Fugue in C minor, for example, takes a (higher pitched than the normal instrument), bassoon and strings (all the concertos have continuo parts). This piece differs from the other five in that it includes dance movements: two minuets and a polacca (Polish dance, moderate triple time). The most adventurous of the Brandenburg Concertos is number 2, which calls for a concertino of high (or piccolo) trumpet, flute (end-blown), oboe and violin. The trumpet part is pitched very high and the problems of balance between these instruments are obvious, but the music is so skilfully written that all soloists have an equal role. This concerto is one of the most brilliant and exciting examples of its kind and, in fact, the Brandenburg Concertos remain outstanding examples of the genre.

Leipzig (1723–50)

Bach's final appointment was Cantor (director of music) at St Thomas's church, Leipzig. His duties included supervising all the music for performance in the various churches of that city, which in practice meant composing many cantatas, sometimes at the rate of one per week. More than 200 cantatas from this period survive, with perhaps the same number lost. Bach had always been a devout Lutheran, and the towering achievement from these years is the music for choir and orchestra: the *Passions* of St Matthew and St John, the *Magnificat* and the *Mass in B minor*. Towards the end of his life, Bach began an ambitious project, *The Art of Fugue*, with the intention of exploring all of the possibilities of the form. No particular instruments were specified and it is not clear whether performance was even intended. Blindness overcame him in 1749, and he underwent an un-successful eye operation. He died the following year, leaving his final work unfinished. Bach married twice, his first wife having died in 1720, and fathered 20 children, of whom nine survived him. We shall meet two of his sons in Chapter 11.

Handel

J. S. Bach and George Frideric Handel (1685–1759) were born in the same year, within 80 miles of each other, but they never met, and were to lead very different lives. Handel's father was a barber-surgeon in Halle, near Leipzig, a position which was not as humble as it may sound. The family was rather better-off than Bach's, and Handel *père* wanted his youngest son to study law, but the boy, so the story goes, had literally been burning the

midnight oil by secretly practising the clavichord (a very small, quiet keyboard instrument) in the attic. His father relented, and the young Handel received lessons in harpsichord, violin, theory and composition.

Hamburg (1703–06)

After a year as assistant organist at the cathedral in Halle, Handel moved to Hamburg in 1703, and was engaged in the orchestra of the opera house, as a violinist initially, then at the harpsichord. This choice of employment highlights the fundamental difference between the interests of Handel and Bach. While Bach remained as a court and church composer, Handel was drawn to the theatre. At Hamburg, his first opera *Almira* (1704) was produced, with some success, which was quite an achievement for a young man not yet 20 years old. But Handel had his sights set on Italy, where he went in 1706, determined to perfect his command of the Italian operatic style.

Italy (1706–10)

He visited the great centres of Italian music: Florence, Rome, Venice and Naples, and for a while was employed by Prince Francesco Ruspoli, in Rome. The music which emerged from the four years Handel spent in Italy proved that he had fully absorbed the idiom. The works include two operas, two oratorios, and perhaps as many as 150 secular cantatas, of which around 100 are extant. During his stay he met many composers including Vivaldi, Corelli, Alessandro Scarlatti and his son Domenico, a brilliant harpsichordist and composer for that instrument, whose single-movement sonatas are well worth an audition. Handel and Scarlatti were brought together one day for a 'trial of skill', after which the consensus seems to have been that Scarlatti was the superior harpsichordist, but the honours for organ playing went to *il Sassone* (the Saxon).

In 1710, Handel returned to Germany and obtained the position of Kapellmeister to the Elector of Hanover, a prestigious post with a relatively high salary. He very quickly obtained leave of absence, and travelled to London, where the fashionable taste for Italian opera meant that he was immediately made welcome by the musical establishment and indeed the court of Queen Anne. He stayed for eight months, during which time his opera *Rinaldo* was staged with great success at the Queen's Theatre in the Haymarket. He returned to

Hanover in 1711, but was back in England the following year, this time to stay. Unfortunately, he did not inform his employer of his intentions, and he was eventually relieved of his position in Hanover.

England (1711–59)

A problem arose for the composer when, in 1714, Queen Anne died, and the Elector of Hanover succeeded to the British throne as George I. Here was a potentially sticky situation for the ex-Kapellmeister, having to face his old boss again. It looked for a while as though Handel had made a serious diplomatic and tactical blunder. But, miraculously, nothing happened – things carried on as before, and Handel soon re-established his reputation with the composition of several fine works in honour of the new king. In 1717 a great water party was held in honour of the king, and a barge with about 50 musicians followed the royal barge, playing a suite 'composed express for this occasion by Mr. Hendel'. The king was so pleased with this 'Water Music' that he 'caused it to be repeated three times in all . . . namely twice before and once after supper'. There was no doubt about Handel's popularity with the king by this time, he soon became teacher to the royal children and by 1723 was composer to the Chapel Royal.

Handel continued to produce operas in Italian style, even after the taste for such entertainments in London began to wane. However, from the early 1730s, he turned increasingly to oratorio. *Esther* (1732 – there had been an earlier version in 1720) was one of the first London oratorios to be staged, followed by 19 others, including the ever popular *Messiah* (1742, first performed in Dublin) and culminating in a reworking of an earlier work *The Triumph of Time and Truth*, performed in 1757, two years before his death. These oratorios were works of great drama and inspiration and were appreciated by Handel's peers as well as the general public. When he heard the Hallelujah Chorus in *Messiah*, Haydn is said to have wept, and declared 'He is the master of us all!'

Handel's musical triumphs were many. Among the operas and oratorios, there are concerti grossi, organ concertos, the coronation anthem *Zadok the Priest*, composed for George II and played at coronations ever since, and the well-known *Music for the Royal Fireworks*, originally celebrating the peace at Aix-la-Chapelle in 1748. The rich seam of Handelian legacy is constantly yielding up gold, as long- forgotten works are revived for the stage. It is ironic that Handel and Bach, after pursuing very different paths in life and music, both died in a state of total blindness after suffering at the hands of the same surgeon.

Handel, unmarried, was given a funeral befitting his celebrity and buried in Westminster Abbey. After Bach's death, his widow was forced to sell his manuscripts to Leipzig city to offset her 'impoverished state'. In Bach and Handel, we have the two giants who closed the Baroque era, different in many respects, but equal in the eyes of posterity.

the Classical era

In this chapter you will learn:

● about another pair of famous names: Haydn and Mozart

● about the Classical style in music, and the changing social status of the composer during this period

● about a formidable new character appearing in the shape of Ludwig van Beethoven.

Even as Bach and Handel were reaching the twin peaks of their achievement, tastes began to change. There was a reaction against the contrapuntal complexities of the Baroque. What was seen as a severe, 'learned' style was gradually rejected in favour of more straightforward, clear lines which were not complicated by the interweaving of several strands of melody that was the Baroque trademark. This particular period has become known as the Age of Enlightenment, and is characterized by values that have their roots in classical antiquity.

The architects of ancient Greece and Rome valued above all the ideals of proportion, symmetry and uncluttered line. Eighteenth-century architects and artists espoused these ideals as the highest achievements of humanity, and sought to emulate them and adapt them to the conditions of their age. Thus the wealthy English had their houses designed on classical lines, as interpreted by the sixteenth-century architect, Palladio, who had published an influential book on the classical style.

These same ideals were applied to music. Greater clarity was sought, and there was a consequent move away from the contrapuntal style of composition. Domenico Scarlatti (1685–1757, a contemporary of Handel and Bach), in his single-movement keyboard sonatas, showed little inclination towards a contrapuntal development of his themes. Johann Sebastian Bach's son Carl Philip Emanuel (1714–88) rejected his father's example, and wrote pieces in the new *galant* style, which reflected the age in its emphasis on elegance and politeness. He played a part in the development of the sonata and the symphony, and was nurtured by composers like Johann Stamitz (1717–57) at the court of Mannhiem. Another of Bach's sons, Johann Christian (1735–82), became known as the 'English Bach', because of his long residence in London, and was said to have been an influence on the young Mozart when he visited the city. At this point, we should pause for a moment and think about the significant differences between the emerging Classical style and its antecedents.

Musical characteristics of the Classical style

The changes made between about 1730 and 1800 set the pattern of forms and practices which were to endure, with some modifications, until the twentieth century.

Apart from the new definitions of sonata, symphony and solo concerto which were beginning to crystalize, there are three other aspects of the new style which should be noted: expression and mood, orchestration and balance.

Expression and mood

The Baroque practice was to sustain a single mood through each movement of a piece, with little variation in dynamics, or tempo or instrumentation. Contrasts of expression became an essential ingredient of the newer music, with emphasis placed on sensitivity, passion and drama.

Orchestration

Because of the essentially contrapuntal nature of Baroque music, there was little distinction made between the roles of the various types of instruments. Melodic lines were freely exchanged between strings, woodwind and brass in the course of contrapuntal movement (remember Bach's Brandenburg Concerto No. 2, where the trumpet, violin, recorder and oboe all interweave, playing similar lines).

The Classical orchestra

In the Classical orchestra the violins take the lion's share of the melodies. Woodwind have a dual role, sometimes supporting or 'doubling' the strings or contributing to the accompanying mix. Horns are useful in their huge melodic and dynamic range, capable of laying down a carpet of sustained chords or adding to the power of the ensemble when necessary. However, the natural (valveless) horns and trumpets of the eighteenth century were restricted in the notes they could play in the lower registers. The trumpets in particular were relegated to playing rhythmic patterns, often in conjunction with the timpani, and adding to the impact of the loud passages. The brilliant, though difficult, high solo parts used to great effect by Bach and Handel, were not required by the Classical composers.

With these massive changes in the use of the orchestra, the continuo became unnecessary, and was eventually dropped, except for opera, where it was needed to accompany recitatives. The orchestra became more or less standardized, with two of each of flutes, oboes, bassoons, horns and trumpets, plus strings and a pair of kettledrums (timpani). The string numbers are rather more variable, but they might be considerably smaller than you would expect, with anything from two to ten each of first and second violins, two to four violas and cellos, and one or two basses.

The major change which took place in the eighteenth century was to use some instruments for accompanying roles, supporting the harmonic framework in various ways, like sustained notes, repeated figures or broken chords. Others might be used to strengthen the melodic lines with their distinctive voices. In other words, composers began to think in terms of instrumental colour and texture.

Balance

Perhaps the single quality that best reflects the Classical ideal is balance. The movements within a symphony were balanced in mood and length, and within the movement the sonata principle ensured a balanced presentation, working out and representation of ideas. To focus even more accurately, the themes were usually built from short, often four-bar phrases. If we think back to our Haydn and Mozart case studies in Part One, we find that in both examples, one four-bar phrase, is answered by another, forming the first musical 'sentence'. The short themes so introduced permeate the whole movement by repetition and development, and thus provide a unifying factor for that section of the work. This contrasts with the Baroque method of developing themes by contrapuntal interaction. One great similarity between the mature Baroque and Classical styles is that both were dominated by two great names. In the Classical era, those names were Haydn and Mozart.

Haydn

Most of the characteristics of the Classical style were in place when Joseph Haydn (1732–1809) began his musical career. The son of a wheelwright, he became a chorister at St Stephen's Cathedral in Vienna at the age of eight, and remained there until his voice broke nine years later. A precarious period of studying followed, with a little teaching to provide a slender income. During this time Haydn played through as many works as he could lay his hands on, including the sonatas of C. P. E. Bach, which he particularly enjoyed. The first professional appointment came in 1759, as director of music to Count Morzin. He stayed for two years during which time he wrote his first symphonies and string quartets. Morzin, a Bohemian, had financial difficulties, and kept only a small orchestra, which had to be disbanded in 1761, and so Haydn was faced with that most modern of problems: redundancy.

In the service of Prince Esterházy (1761–90)

Fortunately, he soon found employment, and, later that same year, he took up the position of assistant Kapellmeister to the Hungarian nobleman Prince Nicolaus Esterházy. Unlike Morzin, Esterházy was extremely wealthy, and Haydn was happy to remain in his employ for the next 30 years. But this first position was not one which carried a high status. Haydn and the musicians under his direction were expected to wear uniform at all times, being classed as members of the household staff, along with the servants, footmen and other employees. Conditions of service included appearing daily to receive instructions from the Prince as to musical performances, and to compose 'such pieces of music as his Serene Princely Highness may command'. These were to be 'wholly for the exclusive use of his Highness', and furthermore, Haydn was forbidden to compose for any occasion outside the estate without prior permission from the Prince. Thus the Esterházys owned Haydn's entire creative output, and left few opportunities for him to make his name independently. In addition to composition, the vice Kapellmeister was responsible for the professional and social conduct of the orchestra, and even the condition of the music and instruments.

Nevertheless, there is evidence that Haydn enjoyed his years with the Esterházy family, and had a particularly warm relationship with Prince Nicholas, who succeeded to the title in 1762. Nicholas was a great music lover and amateur musician, encouraging Haydn (who became Kapellmeister in 1766) to experiment. Haydn is quoted as saying, with evident pride: 'My Prince was always satisfied with my works . . . I was cut off from the world; there was no one to confuse or torment me, and I was forced to be original'. It was only when Prince Nicholas died, in 1790, that Haydn retired from his position and began to travel. An abundance of music flowed from the Esterházy period, including symphonies, concertos, masses, oratorios, operas, divertimentos (sets of short pieces), sonatas, trios and quartets, plus 126 baryton trios. These last works were for the instrument played by Prince Nicholas, which was a curious hybrid, rather like a viola da gamba, with an extra set of strings that were free to vibrate in sympathy with the notes being sounded in the conventional way. A new virtuoso player is required to spearhead a baryton revival, and unlock this treasurehouse of Haydn compositions for baryton, viola and cello.

Visit to England (1790–2)

In 1790, Haydn's life changed dramatically. He accepted an invitation from the impresario, Salomon, to visit England, and to write six new symphonies for performance there. After undertaking the perilous 17-day journey, including a queasy sea voyage, Haydn arrived in England to universal acclaim. The new symphonies were encored and their composer was lionized by the musical establishment and the nobility. The moving performance of *Messiah* (see Chapter 10) took place during this visit, which stretched to a hectic 18 months. The music which came from this last period of Haydn's life, was imbued with the assurance of a mature master at the height of his powers. This is not to say that the earlier works were anything less than excellent. It is difficult, when faced with a corpus of works as extensive and consistent as Haydn's to single out pieces for recommended listening. The symphonies range from the charm of the *galant* to the sophistication of the high Classical style.

Development of the string quartet

Any biographical sketch of Haydn, however brief, must include a note about the development of the string quartet. Whether or not he invented the medium has been the subject of debate. Some scholars insist that Sammartini Giovanni (c.1698–1775) was the first to use a quartet of two violins, viola and cello; others give the credit to Boccerini or Tartini. Be that as it may, the string quartet as used by Haydn (and many composers thereafter) was almost certainly a development of the Italian model of the string trio, adapted to Classical principles. Haydn made the string quartet his own, and was certainly the first composer to appreciate and fully exploit its sonorous and intimate qualities. A large number of composers have chosen the quartet to express their most profound musical thoughts. The Classical string quartet takes the form of a sonata in four movements.

Second visit to London (1794)

Haydn made a second triumphal visit to London in 1794, when he was again feted and this time was presented to King George III. The second set of 'Salomon symphonies' dates from this period (again of 18 months), as well as three piano sonatas, and numerous songs, including arrangements of Scottish folk songs. On his return to Austria, Haydn embarked on what were to be his final works. Not surprisingly, he turned again to the string quartet with a set of six quartets, Op. 76 and Op. 77 (two quartets). The final quartet, Op. 103 (1801), remained unfinished.

The Creation

The crowning glory of Haydn's life, though not his final work, was the great oratorio *The Creation*. Always a devout man, Haydn's experience of Handel's works in London inspired him to set passages from Milton translated into German. The result is a true successor to the Handelian oratorio: perfection in orchestral and choral writing and great dramatic impact. The composer heard a performance of the work the year before he died and was visibly moved. When the choir and orchestra exploded into glorious sound on the word *Licht* (light), Haydn looked upward and said helplessly 'Not from me – it came from above'. It was typical of Haydn to disown his contribution, but he left behind a legacy of work of consistently high quality, and established a number of new forms which were continued for many generations to come. If we think of Bach and Handel as closing an era, then Haydn certainly held open the door for the next.

Mozart

Genius is a problematical word; it is impossible to define. You could say (with some justification) that Haydn was touched by genius, but then, by the same token, Wolfgang Amadeus Mozart (1756–91) was saturated with it. The ever-modest Haydn said of Mozart: 'friends often flatter me that I have some genius, but he stood far above me.' To say Mozart was a child prodigy is an understatement – he was *the* child prodigy, undoubtedly the most naturally gifted composer the world has ever seen. At the age of six he was taken, with his sister (who was five years his senior), on a tour of the great palaces of the royalty and aristocracy of Europe, showing off the extraordinary talents of the *Wunderkinde*. When he was eight, he was constructing sonatas and fugues with J. C. Bach in London, and by the time he was nine, he had composed his first symphony. This may seem to us to be an appalling example of exploitation of children, but there is little doubt that their father, Leopold, had what he sincerely believed to be the children's best interests at heart.

Leopold Mozart was a violinist and composer (later Vice Kapellmeister) in the service of Prince Archbishop of Salzburg, and his ambition was to procure the most lucrative possible court appointment for his brilliant son. The only way to advertise Wolfgang's existence was to parade him before the people of influence. But Wolfgang was not destined to follow his father's, or Haydn's way of life, as an employee of a grand patron, with all the restrictions that implies. He did accept one appointment, in 1779 as court organist to his father's employer, but was dismissed two years later and moved to Vienna. The freelance life was not without precedent, after all Handel was self-employed for most of his professional career. But Mozart lacked Handel's entrepreneurial skills, and he was constantly dogged with financial problems, although his music betrays none of this insecurity, bubbling over with infectious enthusiasm for life.

Dissonance

Mozart's complete command of every musical idiom produced works of absolute perfection, the height of the Classical ideal of taste. Not all of his contemporaries would have agreed with this, though; they found some of his harmonic adventures to be discordant and ugly. Take for example the set of six string quartets (1782–5) dedicated to Haydn, for whom Mozart always had the highest regard, and especially No. 19, nicknamed the 'Dissonance' (discord). In Mozart's day these were challenging, modern pieces. Because fairly remote keys are explored in the development sections, some members of Mozart's audience recoiled from the unfamiliar sounds and condemned the music. This is something we should all bear in mind when listening to contemporary music today. What may seem to be unacceptably discordant may be merely unfamiliar and might on further listening become interesting and even enjoyable.

This is not to say that all Mozart's music was unsuccessful, the operas *The Marriage of Figaro* and *Don Giovanni* were produced to some acclaim in Prague, though not in Mozart's adopted home of Vienna where they were considered to be too dissonant for the delicate Viennese taste. Unfortunately for Mozart, no system of royalties or profit sharing was available to him, and he was paid only a single fee for the composition of the operas, regardless of the number of performances that might be given. Nor was there any system of copyright for music, so anyone was free to publish and perform works as they pleased, for which the composer would receive no payment whatsoever. Therefore two of Mozart's greatest and most successful operas netted only small fees and no recognition of his success at home. They did not solve any financial problems.

Prodigious output

Mozart wrote a total of 11 operas, both serious and comic, plus five *Singspiele*, one of which was unfinished. These last are comic works with spoken dialogue, in German, as distinct from the operas, which were in the Italian demanded by the conventions of the time. The best-known, and most successful, *Singspiel* is *The Magic Flute* (1791), which, ironically, became widely popular only after the composer's death. In his short life, Mozart produced an incredible amount of music, including 41 symphonies, 21 piano concertos, plus concertos for other instruments like violin, clarinet, flute and horn, 23 string quartets, 17 piano sonatas and various combinations of chamber music. There is not the space here for a complete list, but this task of cataloguing Mozart's prodigious output was painstakingly undertaken, and published in 1862, by Ludwig Köchel. His system of numbering of Mozart's works is still used, though it has been revised several times since the first edition. You will almost always see in the title of a Mozart piece, the 'K' number by which it can be identified, for example: Symphony No. 40 in G minor, K550. More recently, other composers have been given the same treatment by researchers and cataloguers. Haydn has a Hoboken number (HOB) and Domenico Scarlatti's is Kirkpatrick (Kk), but Köchel is the only one which is universally recognised and quoted, to date.

The last three symphonies are truly extraordinary, written during a creative burst that was exceptional even by Mozart's standard. In a period of about eight weeks between June and August 1788, symphonies 39–41 (K543, K550 and K551) emerged from Mozart's fertile imagination. There is no record of their having been performed during his lifetime, nor were they published. Moreover, the composer was going through one of the worst periods of his life, suffering the loss of a young child, as well as extreme penury. Despite this, the symphonies turned out to be the most sublime examples of their kind, running the gamut of emotional expression, with the perfection of form which makes them superb examples of the mature Classical style.

The final symphony, the 'Jupiter', features in its closing movement a supremely assured essay in contrapuntal writing, demonstrating Mozart's understanding and

Mozart, on his death-bed, working on his Requiem

mastery of earlier techniques. It's worth noting that Haydn's later symphonies bear the influence of the younger man, Mozart having repaid the debt to his musical mentor.

Mozart's death

There is no foundation to the story of Mozart's being poisoned by the rival composer Antonio Salieri, which originally appeared in a poem by Pushkin (1830) and formed the basis of an opera by Rimsky-Korsakov in 1898, as well as the more recent play and film *Amadeus* by Peter Schaffer. However, in 1791 a Requiem was commissioned by an anonymous client, and Mozart, suffering from stress and depression, imagined that the Requiem was to be his own. He became seriously ill, but continued to compose the Requiem, dictating the orchestral and choral parts to his pupil, Franz Süssmeyr. Mozart carried on dictating the music from his death-bed, but was unable to finish it. Süssmeyr completed the Requiem, and it remains one of the most poignantly beautiful examples of its kind. Mozart was buried in an unmarked pauper's grave. The handful of mourners who attended were discouraged by a sudden violent storm, so the burial took place without witnesses. Haydn was in

London at the time, and the news of Mozart's death came as a terrible shock to him. He wrote to Mozart's widow Constanze, offering such help as he was able to give.

Beethoven – the early years

The following year (1792), on his way home from London, Haydn stopped in Bonn and was entertained by the orchestra of the Elector of Cologne. Haydn also met a young viola player from the orchestra and agreed to take him as a pupil in Vienna. This was Ludwig van Beethoven (1770–1827), of whom Mozart had said five years before: 'Keep your eyes on him. Some day he will give the world something to talk about.' Soon after, Beethoven left for Vienna, which became his home for the rest of his life. The ever generous Haydn lent Beethoven some money and wrote to the Elector asking for a small allowance to be paid to the young man. Haydn may have had in mind his own impoverished years in the city, and he treated Beethoven with great kindness, both personally and as a teacher. In some ways this was not the best thing for the headstrong young pupil, who eventually sought a stricter training in the techniques of counterpoint with more exacting, but less imaginative teachers like Albrechtsberger and Salieri.

Beethoven acquired a loose sort of employment, involving board, lodging and a small income, from the music-loving Prince Lichnowsky, who had a great deal of regard for the composer's music, and was considerate enough to instruct his servants to answer Beethoven's bell before his own. But Beethoven was a free spirit, who rejected the patronage of the nobility, though he would accept commissions and provide dedications, like, for example, the three Piano Trios, Op. 1 which are dedicated to Prince Lichnowsky. He also became known as a professional pianist of astonishing ability, but would often refuse requests to perform at private gatherings.

By the turn of the century, Beethoven had the musical world at his feet. He was established as a virtuoso pianist, and his reputation as a composer was growing, with plenty of commissions to keep him financially secure. His first symphony was performed in 1800, and among other works, the third piano concerto and six string quartets, Op. 18 were completed. At this time, just when everything seemed to be going his way, the greatest possible tragedy struck; he began to lose his hearing. By 1802, it had become apparent that the condition was progressive and incurable. Beethoven shunned company and sought solace in the countryside. He was 32 years old.

the Romantics

In this chapter you will learn:

- the continuation of Beethoven's story, together with that of the major Romantic composers who followed him

- about the development of opera as it flourished across Europe in the nineteenth century.

Beethoven – the agent of change

Beethoven finally came to terms with his tragic disability, and from his country retreat in Heiligenstadt wrote a moving document addressed to his brothers, to be read after his death. He confesses that he had contemplated suicide, but had resisted the urge because of his art:

Ah, it seemed to me to be impossible to leave the world before I had brought forth all that I was destined to bring forth. So I endured this miserable existence – miserable indeed.

This has become known as the Heiligenstadt Testament, and it reveals a Beethoven in 1802, resigned to his fate, but aware of the obligations of his gifts. Two years later he completed his monumental Third Symphony, the 'Eroica'.

The 'Eroica' Symphony

The first two symphonies are very much in the Classical mould as far as construction and proportion are concerned, although some of the themes are distinctly 'Beethovenian' in character, but the 'Eroica' is the product of a much grander conception. It is about twice

Beethoven, from a portrait by J. W. Mähler (c.1804)

the length of a Haydn/Mozart symphony, and the first movement is far more adventurous than anything that had been attempted before. The development section is particularly extended, making full use of exposition themes, but also introducing new material. An extended coda also prolongs the working of the thematic material, which did not please some of the audience at the first performance. One critic observed that: 'This long, extremely difficult composition . . . very often seems to lose itself in anarchy.' Another concluded that: 'for the audience the symphony was too difficult [and] too long.'

It seems appropriate at this point to mention the well-known story of the Third Symphony's popular title. Beethoven had great sympathy with the growth of democracy in France, and consequently was an admirer of Napoleon Bonaparte, to whom he dedicated this revolutionary new symphony. On hearing that Napoleon had declared himself Emperor, according to an eye-witness, Beethoven 'seized the score, tore off the title page and threw it on the floor, all the while cursing the new Emperor of the French as the "new tyrant"'. The composer eventually consented to the title *Sinfonia Eroica* (Heroic Symphony), subtitled 'composed to celebrate the memory of a great man'.

Romantic interpretation

The second movement of the 'Eroica' is a funeral march, which presents a problem for a programmatic interpretation of the symphony, as Beethoven seems to have killed off his hero. Moreover, the movement is followed by a hectic scherzo, Beethoven's trademark since the Second Symphony (even in the First Symphony the 'minuet' is taken at quite a speed). The positioning of the scherzo after the funeral march is difficult to explain, although one or two commentators have tried. Berlioz, for example, suggested that it represented 'funeral games around the grave of the warrior, such as those in the *Iliad*'. The finale comprises ten variations on a theme from the ballet *The Creatures of Prometheus*, so we might assume that by this stage the central figure is Prometheus himself, the mythical hero and benefactor of mankind.

The above is a Romantic way of interpreting a symphony. Before Beethoven, the general view was that music served a utilitarian purpose, composed for a specific function be it religious or recreational, church or court. Perhaps Mozart's last symphonies were the earliest

examples of a new freedom of expression that could be called Romantic. The 'Eroica' was a great step forward in this process, and had a profound effect on the expressive function of the symphony. The movement was away from the intellectual to the emotional, from the head to the heart, a movement that was mirrored in nineteenth-century literature with poets like Goethe and Schiller in Germany, Byron and Shelley in England.

Three periods

It is common practice to divide Beethoven's work into three periods, early, middle and late; the 'Eroica' being an example of the middle period. You may think this is rather an artificial and arbitrary distinction, but as you read more about Beethoven, you will certainly come across references to the three periods, so a few signposts for categorization would be useful. As you will have surmised from the information above, the onset of deafness around 1800 divides the first and second periods. If we restrict our survey to the major instrumental forms of piano sonata, string quartet and symphony, we should get a picture of where the divisions between the three periods lie.

Early: piano sonatas Op. 2–28, string quartets Op. 18, Symphonies 1 and 2.
Middle: piano sonatas Op. 31–90, string quartets Op. 59 (Rasoumovsky Quartets) –95, Symphonies 3–8.
Late: piano sonatas Op. 101–111, string quartets Op. 127–135 (and the *Grosse Fuge*), Symphony No. 9.

I realize that this is a very basic list, with no mention of the concertos, much chamber music, *Missa Solemnis* (late), or Beethoven's one opera *Fidelio* (middle), but I hope that, by listening to works from all three periods, you will recognize the broad stylistic differences between the three periods. If you would like to see a complete list of Beethoven's compositions (or those of any composer), your local library will probably have a set of the multi-volume *Grove's Dictionary of Music and Musicians*, which provides details of all the works.

The Ninth Symphony

Although it is quite useful to pigeon-hole Beethoven's works into three separate sections, we mustn't forget that each represents a stage in the progression of the creative life of the artist. The Ninth Symphony (1824) would not have been possible without the Third and Fifth, nor, for that matter, the First. Rather than being a 'one-off' piece of sublime inspiration, the Ninth was the culmination of all Beethoven's symphonic ideas, and it was probably the most influential work of the nineteenth century. Hardly a composer who followed was untouched by it. In the Ninth Symphony (the subtitle 'Choral' was only ever adopted in Britain, and seems now to be falling from favour), Beethoven showed that the symphonic form was capable of sustaining a previously unimaginable length and range of emotional ideas.

The first movement is as long as a whole symphony of Haydn or Mozart, beginning, like the 'Eroica' and the Fifth, with a very simple opening theme, a descending two-note motif, which is introduced by the first violins over **tremolando** strings and a sustained chord in the horns. The effect is one of breathless anticipation, described by the composer and critic Robert Simpson as 'like the genesis of music itself'. It continues for 16 bars, the violins teasing us with snatches of the melody, until the whole orchestra crashes in at bar 17 with the completed downward **arpeggio** which begins the theme, and movement proper. The great dramatic control of the mature master never falters throughout the long first movement which is followed by a bouncing scherzo, with off-beat timpani accents. Then follows the poignant slow movement, reversing the position of the inner two movements in the 'Eroica', and thus avoiding the problem of shattering the contemplative mood with a scherzo.

The finale of the Ninth Symphony is the most breathtakingly original part of an already audacious work. After a slightly chaotic fanfare (woodwind, brass and timpani), cellos and basses perform a series of recitatives, as though discussing the material that has been presented to them. In between these, the orchestra plays the opening bars of each of the proceeding movements. Beethoven is unifying his unprecedentedly long symphony by introducing thematic material from earlier movements into the finale, a practice which many later symphonists adopted. The cellos and basses seem to reject each of the previous themes with acerbic recitatives, until a new theme is begun, quietly, by the woodwind. This is accepted and played through by the lower strings, and then gradually taken up by the full orchestra. This single theme dominates the finale in various forms.

Beethoven's orchestra

The orchestra demanded by Beethoven for the Ninth Symphony required some additions to the basic Classical format that we examined in Chapter 11. Double woodwind (two each of flutes, oboes and bassoons) includes two clarinets (standard since late Mozart), plus piccolo and contra-bassoon, extending the range of the woodwind at both ends. The brass section comprises two trumpets, four horns and three trombones (these had first appeared in the Fifth Symphony), Percussion now sported triangle, cymbals and bass drum, in addition to the normal timpani.

After a reprise of the opening fanfare, the music is interrupted by the solo baritone, who intones in a recitative: 'O friends, not these sounds! Let us raise a song of sympathy and gladness, O Joy, let us praise thee!' He then sings a setting of Schiller's *Ode to Joy*, a poem dedicated to the ideal of the brotherhood of man. The chorale-like theme now becomes a hymn to Joy, ending:

All mankind are brother plighted
Where thy gentle wings abide.

The theme is taken through many variations, with solo soprano, alto, tenor and baritone voices and chorus, plus instrumental episodes and accompaniments including a double **fugato** (passage in fugal style within a non-fugal movement), and a Turkish march (slightly exotic effect, with wind and percussion only). These last devices had been employed in the finale of the 'Eroica', though not in such dramatic form. The Ninth Symphony represents the consummation of Beethoven's musical and philosophical ideas, and sets the symphonic agenda for the rest of the century.

Schubert

We saw in the previous two chapters that the eighteenth century was dominated by a handful of great names. In contrast, the following hundred years saw an explosion of diverse activity, with new innovators pushing out the boundaries in all directions. If we look first at those who were closest to the influence of Beethoven, we must begin with Franz Schubert (1797–1828), who died tragically young, but achieved much during his brief lifetime. Schubert, like Beethoven, links the Classical and Romantic eras. His earlier symphonies, though lively and tuneful, are reminiscent of Mozart, but the last two, No. 8 (the 'Unfinished', 1822) and No. 9 (the 'Great' C major, 1828) demonstrate an ability to create and sustain dramatic interest over an extended form. Unfortunately, Symphony No. 8 presented difficulties that proved to be insurmountable for the young composer.

The problem of the 'Unfinished' Symphony

After two perfectly constructed movements, Schubert seemed to run out of steam. There is a piano sketch of a scherzo, but it was never completed. The reason for this will never be known, but possibly Schubert lacked the confidence as a symphonist to complete the work. If he was unhappy with the scherzo, it is unlikely that he would have been able to imagine a convincing finale, with the example of Beethoven looming large before him. There has been a theory postulated that the **entr'acte** in B minor from the incidental music to *Rosamunde* (1823) could be the missing finale from the 'Unfinished', as there are some melodic similarities between it and the scherzo music.

There is no documentary evidence to substantiate this theory, because Schubert left no sketches for a finale as he did for the first two movements and the incomplete scherzo. It is more likely that he salvaged some ideas from the abandoned scherzo and used them for the *Rosamunde* music, one of the few professional commissions that he was to receive. Furthermore, if the entr'acte was ever considered for the finale of the 'Unfinished', it is easy to see why Schubert changed his mind. Though an attractive piece, it is hardly strong enough to complete the work we know from the first two movements. We have to conclude that, unless a completed manuscript has been lost, Schubert was unwilling or unable to solve his problem, and simply abandoned the symphony. It was never performed during his lifetime. Fortunately, we have the 'Great' C major Symphony No. 9, as evidence that Schubert overcame all the difficulties of constructing a symphony on a large scale.

Lieder

One of Schubert's greatest gifts was a seemingly unending stream of melodic invention, which is evident in all his works, but manifests itself most immediately in his songs, of which there are more than 600. Written for voice and piano, in the tradition of German *Lieder* (literally 'songs'), these priceless gems are the spontaneous outpourings of Schubert's response to romantic poetry of

all sorts. Though the poetry may sometimes have been indifferent, the music was never less than inspired. He would write astonishingly quickly, up to eight songs in a day, for evening performance by his wide circle of friends, drawn from the artistic community in Vienna. The Schubertian lieder tradition was carried on by Schumann, Brahms, Hugo Wolf and Richard Strauss, always distinguished by the musical evocation of the poetic mood, and the partnership of voice and piano.

Schubert produced nearly 1,000 works (catalogued by O. E. Deutsch) in his short life, among which are some of the finest chamber works ever to be written. If you're a newcomer to Schubert, apart from the symphonies and songs, you could try the String Quintet (quartet plus extra cello) in C major, the 'Trout' Quintet, any of the 15 string quartets or the piano sonatas. It is tragic to think that many of his greatest works were never performed during his lifetime and that Schubert never earned enough from his compositions to sustain himself. Most depressing of all is to think what great music he might have composed had he lived a little longer.

Mendelssohn

The backgrounds of Schubert and Mendelssohn were vastly different. Schubert's father was a respectable but impecunious schoolmaster, while Felix Mendelssohn (1809–47) came from a family of wealthy Berlin bankers. He was precociously talented, and played a major part in the private concerts that were regularly held at the family house, along with his brother, two sisters and various visiting musicians who were invited to participate. Mendelssohn was content always to work within established forms and has sometimes been dismissed as lacking in depth. In fact, he may have been the victim of his own astounding abilities – he made it look too easy. His works have an almost Mozart-like perfection of design which may sometimes seem facile. It is only necessary to listen to the beautiful and ever popular Violin Concerto to appreciate the emotional and dramatic depth that can be found within an exquisitely wrought piece. The six string quartets deserve to be listened to, as does all the chamber music for strings and the five symphonies, especially the 'Italian', No. 4, and the 'Reformation', No. 5, in which Mendelssohn experiments with modifications of the symphonic structure.

We have already considered, in Chapters 05 and 07, the essentially Romantic tone painting in the *Hebrides* and

Midsummer Night's Dream overtures. It should also be remembered that Mendelssohn had a great interest in the works of earlier composers, particularly J. S. Bach, whose work had been largely forgotten by the public. In 1829, the 20-year-old Mendelssohn conducted the first public performance of the *St Matthew Passion* since Bach's time. Mendelssohn was also a keen contrapuntalist himself, and between 1832 and 1837 wrote nine preludes and fugues, six for piano and three for organ, demonstrating his mastery of that difficult form.

Schumann

One of the characteristics of the Romantics was a tendency to rationalize and describe their aesthetic aims in print, as well as in music. Robert Schumann (1810–56), the son of a bookseller and author, and admirer of Mendelssohn, became a journalist as well as pianist and composer. In 1834, he founded his *New Journal for Music*, a bold venture for the time, and during the next two decades, used its pages to advance the cause of romanticism in music. Schumann also drew attention in his journalism to any new talent he thought deserving. Of many young composers who drew praise from his pen, the two outstanding prophesies of greatness are Chopin ('Hats off gentlemen, a genius') and Brahms, who lived for a time with Schumann and his wife, Clara.

Schumann's own music centres on the piano. His earlier ambition had been to be a virtuoso pianist, until a hand injury (possibly exacerbated by unwise finger exercises) extinguished any possibility of a solo career. Having married his teacher's daughter (against her father's wishes), he had every reason to concentrate on composition. Clara, who was an outstanding pianist, in turn gave definitive performances of her husband's works, as well as being a gifted teacher and composer. In addition to piano pieces, Schumann produced an abundance of songs, a staggering 15 sets (about 120 songs) in the year of his marriage alone. His four symphonies have been criticized for being pianistic rather than orchestral in concept. It is true that Schumann lacked Mendelssohn's polished facility in matters of orchestration, but the symphonies are imbued with an earnest sincerity, and the last of them particularly points forward in terms of organization of musical material.

A major development in Romantic orchestral music, again rooted in Beethoven, is the technique of thematic transformation, which simply means the recurrence of themes, in altered forms, throughout the duration of a piece, rather than confined within a single movement. This was a method of binding together, or unifying, works which were becoming increasingly extended. His Fourth Symphony (1851), was a pioneering work in this field, being largely based on two short themes. Three years after its publication Robert Schumann threw himself into the Rhine. He had been suffering from mental instability for some time, and was committed to an institution for the remainder of his life.

His pregnant wife was consoled by, among others, their young protégé, Johannes Brahms. Clara undertook concert tours with Joseph Joachim, the violinist, to maintain her home and family of seven children, and Brahms came along too. It soon became apparent from his letters that he had fallen in love with Clara, who was 14 years his senior. After Robert's death in 1856, however, feelings cooled and Brahms moved away to take up an old-fashioned appointment as choirmaster and teacher at the court of the Prince of Lippe-Detmold, a post which left plenty of time for composition. But this was 1856, and a young composer was not about to devote his career to servitude in the eighteenth-century manner. Clara Schumann, remained a friend and enthusiastic promoter of Brahms's music for the rest of her life.

Brahms

Johannes Brahms (1833–97) is often described as a conservative composer, and there is some justification for this. His musical vocabulary was that of Schumann, though the two were a generation apart, and he was cautious about embarking upon types of composition which might provoke critical comparison with a distinguished predecessor. Brahms did not, for example, publish a symphony or string quartet until he was over 40, as the shadow of Beethoven loomed large over both of those forms. He did write chamber music in the earlier years, as well as works for solo piano, and the perceptive Schumann pointed out that Brahms had an essentially orchestral style. The sonatas, he said, were 'really disguised symphonies'. The *German Requiem*, composed in 1866, using texts from Luther's translation of the Bible, was the first large-scale work, receiving its first complete performance in 1868. When the First Symphony finally appeared, in 1876, it was immediately dubbed 'Beethoven's Tenth', by some commentators, because the theme in the finale was reminiscent of the 'Ode to Joy' theme in the last movement of Beethoven's Ninth Symphony. Brahms's reply to this was dismissive: 'Any ass can see that!' he declared, forestalling any further discussion.

Brahms has often suffered unfavourable comparison with Beethoven, which is unfair, as the two men were very different temperamentally; a fact that is reflected in their music. Brahms was always thorough and methodical in the working out of his musical ideas. His music can be exciting and innovative, lacking only Beethoven's sheer audacity and ability to surprise listeners with the totally unexpected. But this is a tough act for any artist to follow, and it is to Brahms's credit that he did not attempt to do so, but concentrated instead on forging his own individual style. The subsequent three symphonies move away from the Beethovenian example, and are interesting for their Brahmsian qualities. For example, in the finale of the Fourth Symphony, Brahms employs a Baroque form, the **passacaglia** (originally a dance form in triple time with variations over a ground bass). This work, which had puzzled critics (often a good sign) and some of Brahms's friends, was soon accepted by the public. At a performance in Vienna in March 1897, the ailing composer appeared in public for the last time. A month later he was dead, and the Classical-Romantic style of which he was one of the last exponents drew to a close.

Other Romantics

You will have noticed that we have been tracing the Romantic movement as part of the very important Austro-German musical tradition. Vienna was considered to be the musical capital of the world for more than two centuries. However, there were, as you might expect, composers working outside that tradition, whose explorations took a different direction.

Berlioz

Paris was an exciting and turbulent place to be in the nineteenth century, and the streets were in turmoil in 1830 when the *Symphonie Fantastique* was first performed. Hector Berlioz (1803–69), like the German Romantics, was profoundly influenced by the music of Beethoven, but was not bound by the conventions of Classical (Austro-German) symphonic forms. The *Symphonie Fantastique* may not have been possible without the 'Eroica', Fifth and 'Pastoral' symphonies, but the orchestral technique belongs to Berlioz. In his last two symphonies, *Romeo and Juliet* and *Symphonie funèbre et triomphale* (commissioned by the French government to mark the tenth anniversary of the 1830 Revolution), Berlioz followed the example of Beethoven's Ninth Symphony, and introduced a chorus, although neither work can be said to be stylistically reminiscent of Beethoven.

Liszt

Franz Liszt (1811–86) was also a resident of Paris during the same period. His contribution to the development of piano music goes hand in hand with his career as virtuoso pianist. Clara Schumann, who was not given to hyperbole, declared Liszt to be without equal as a pianist, and admitted that 'he arouses fright and astonishment'. His compositions for piano, including two concertos, are extremely different and always dramatic, even though some of them were designated study pieces. Liszt's interest in the poetic, which we considered earlier (Chapter 06) in relation to his orchestral music, was also apparent in many of the piano works, but there is one massive single-movement sonata, which is dedicated to Schumann.

Chopin

Another adopted Parisian was the Polish-born Frédéric Chopin (1810–49), who impressed the *salons* (gatherings, in private houses, of artists, intellectuals and the fashionable élite) of the city with his pianistic abilities and boldly original compositions. Chopin was taken up by Liszt, who admired his music and introduced him to the female novelist George Sand, with whom he later lived. Even Chopin, a talented pianist himself, said of Liszt 'I should like to steal from him the way to play my own *études*'. Chopin is best known as a miniaturist, for short piano pieces like the **ballades**, **nocturnes**, **Polonaises** and **Mazurkas**, these two last being based on folk-tunes of his native Poland. Nevertheless, he was perfectly capable of working in more extended forms, and produced three sonatas and two concertos, although, unlike Liszt, he disliked performing them in public. He was able to squeeze a wealth of melodic and especially harmonic invention into even his shortest works, and with his delicacy of touch, he extended the expressive range of the piano far beyond any of his contemporaries. Chopin died of tuberculosis at the tragically early age of 39.

Romantic opera

In the first half of the nineteenth century, the development of opera proceeded to a great extent on national lines. The Italian tradition was carried forward by Gioacchino Rossini (1792–1868), Vincenzo Bellini (1801–35) and Gaetano Donizetti (1797–1848). The emphasis remained in the solo song or aria, sung with the emphasis on quality of tone and phrasing, a style which became known as **bel canto** (literally, 'beautiful song'). Recitatives became less stark, now accompanied by orchestra rather than a single keyboard instrument. There was a preference for comic plots furnished with the type of instantly appealing melodies that Rossini seemed to turn out effortlessly in *The Barber of Seville* (1816), *William Tell* (1829) and many others. There are exceptions to this, such as Donizetti's *Lucia di Lammermoor* (1835) which is based on Sir Walter Scott's novel *The Bride of Lammermoor* and contains a superbly dramatic and justly famous 'mad' scene. Operas like *Lucia*, Bellini's *Norma* (1831) and many by Rossini, are tremendously popular today. They are often in the repertoires of touring companies so it's worth keeping an eye open for the possibility of local performances.

Italy

Italian opera in the second half of the nineteenth century is dominated by one name. The works of Giuseppi Verdi (1813–1901) form the mainstay of the world's great opera houses. In his operas, the Italian style reaches its zenith, with a great awareness of dramatic effect, a mastery of the orchestra and a new seriousness of intent. There is not space here for detailed discussion of the individual operas, but the names of a few are enough to indicate the importance of the status of these works in the operatic repertoire. *Rigoletto* (1851), *Il Trovatore* (1853), *La Traviata* (1853), *Aida* (1871), *Otello* (1887) and *Falstaff* (1893) give a rough sketch-map of his mature works; all indispensable operatic favourites in which the works of writers such as Victor Hugo, Alexander Dumas and Shakespeare are exploited for their maximum dramatic content.

France

The French taste for drama on a large scale resulted in the development of *grand opéra* in Paris. A large orchestra and cast, plus spectacular stage effects were demanded by Parisian audiences, and correspondingly large musical concepts were necessary to satisfy this need. Ironically, it was German-born composer, Giacomo Meyerbeer (1791–1864, originally Jakob Liebmann Beer) who was most successful with lavishly staged productions like *Robert le Diable* (1831) and *Les Huguenots* (1836). Berlioz conceived *The Trojans* as an opera on a grand scale, but he was never to see the complete opera performed. Part Two, *The Trojans at Carthage*, was produced during his lifetime, however (in 1863), and did provide enough income from its 21 performances to free him from the necessity of musical journalism, in which he had been engaged for 30 years and professed to despise. It is interesting to note that there was now a system of royalty payments (Berlioz mentions them specifically), which would have saved Mozart from penury and humiliation had they been available in his lifetime.

Germany and Austria

In Germany and Austria, there was not the strong operatic tradition that existed elsewhere. You will remember that the operas of Mozart were sung in Italian, the more Germanic idiom being the *Singspiel*, typified by works like *The Magic Flute*. Carl Maria von Weber (1786–1826) brought the world of German Romantic literature to the *Singspiel* in 1821, with *Der Freischütz* (The Marksman), a tale of dark deeds in a German forest. The hero is induced to obtain some magic bullets, in order to win a shooting contest and gain the hand of the forester's daughter. In the ghostly Wolf's Glen, the bullets are cast by an evil spirit, and as each one is made, a new apparition appears to frighten the hero, until the spirit threatens to possess him. Incredibly (this *is* opera), there is a happy ending to the story, provided by Weber's librettist, who rejected the tragic ending of the original folk-tale.

The music is splendidly evocative of the rustic pleasures of the huntsman and the forester, with much use of the horn (a favourite instrument of the German Romantics). The mysterious and supernatural elements in Act Two are also fully exploited by Weber, whose dramatic sense never wavers, heightening the effect of the spectral events on the stage. Wagner absorbed the influence of this sort of German romanticism, and the expansive ideas of French grand opera, together with the symphonic techniques of Beethoven, to realize his vision of music-drama. We have already encountered that concept and its massive products in Chapter 06. In Chapter 13, we shall see what became of romanticism after Wagner in Austria and Germany, and look at some alternative developments in other countries.

later Romantics and nationalists

In this chapter you will learn:

● about musical development up to the beginning of the twentieth century, travelling across Russia and Europe, beginning with the followers of Wagner in the Austro-German tradition, and the expansion of the orchestra to accommodate their expanded Romantic concepts.

To his followers, Wagner's influence was all-encompassing. His theories of a total aesthetic were presented in publications with titles like *The Art Work of the Future*, expounding large ideas about art and nature, the ancient Greeks, German mythology and Romantic philosophy. But Wagner was first and foremost a musician, and in this area his authority was most effective. In his operas, the orchestra was of equal status to the performers; he was essentially a tone-poet, like Berlioz and Liszt, but on a larger scale. Moreover, he altered the existing harmonic vocabulary, using chords which did not 'follow on' in the traditional way. Such harmonic ambiguity enabled him to extend his musical thoughts to new boundaries, further from the 'home' key than had been acceptable before.

Bruckner

Although Wagner wrote little apart from opera, he was indirectly responsible for extending the Austro-German symphonic tradition, because the symphonists who followed him were deeply influenced by his musical ideas. Anton Bruckner (1824–96) was a great admirer of Wagner, always referring to him as 'the Master'. Bruckner was as modest and self-effacing as Wagner was bold and confident (even arrogant). Like Brahms, his near contemporary, Bruckner did not publish a symphony until he was over 40, in fact, he deemed his first symphony unworthy to be classified as such and it now bears the title 'number 0'. Bruckner took manuscripts of his Second and Third symphonies to Wagner seeking the great man's approval. Wagner chose the Third, and Bruckner was so overawed that, when he left, he forgot which work Wagner had preferred. He scribbled a hasty note to the maestro which is still preserved (a rare document containing the signatures of both men), to check that he had the correct symphony to dedicate to Wagner. The Third Symphony is in the same key as Beethoven's Ninth and its opening theme is reminiscent of the earlier work.

Bruckner always used his melodic material to hold together what became very large structures (the Eighth Symphony lasts about an hour and a half). The first and last movements contain related themes, and this overarching structure gives a sense of balance and cohesion to the whole work. The symphonies have been called 'cathedrals of sound', and indeed their architecture is conceived on a grand scale. But there is a pleasing straightforwardness about the music, which reveals the composer's fundamental honesty and naive charm. After a successful rehearsal of the Fourth Symphony, the

'Romantic', Bruckner approached the internationally famous conductor Hans Richter and slipped a coin into his hand for a post-concert drink. This personality is reflected in the inner movements of the symphonies particularly, in the earthy swing of the scherzos (often based on *Ländler*, a rustic Austrian dance) and the ethereal beauty of the slow movements, imbued with an almost spiritual intensity. Bruckner was a man of great religious faith, and, apart from the symphonies, some of his greatest works were settings of sacred texts like the mighty *Te Deum*, which he once suggested could serve as the finale for his unfinished Ninth Symphony.

Mahler

Gustav Mahler (1860–1911) came to know Bruckner at the Vienna Conservatory, where, as a student, he greatly admired the older man's work. Mahler's early reputation was made as a conductor, at first in small theatres and opera houses. Then, on a recommendation from Brahms, he was given a conducting post at the Vienna Opera, where he later became artistic director. He also accepted invitations to conduct all over Europe, as well as Russia and America, and so became one of the first of a new breed of cosmopolitan conductors, whose descendants can been seen in the jet-setting 'superstar' conductors of today. He was a composer at heart, however, and holidays were always spent working on new compositions, at a lakeside family retreat. He managed to produce a good corpus of work in this way, including nine symphonies (since Beethoven, this number seems to have a special significance, Schubert, Bruckner and Dvořák all composed nine symphonies) and an unfinished tenth, plus songs with orchestral accompaniment. These two forms coincide in the Second, Third and Fourth symphonies, and *Das Lied von der Erde* (The Song of the Earth), which Mahler insisted was to be thought of as a symphony. The idea of a choral finale, begun by Beethoven in the Ninth Symphony, is extended by Mahler in the 'Symphony of a Thousand', No. 8, and *Das Lied von der Erde*, commemorating the death of his elder daughter, is a valedictory piece for Mahler himself, and perhaps for the Austro-German romanticism of which it is a late example.

Until the 1950s, Mahler's music was hardly played outside Germany and Austria, but since the 1960s there has been an explosion of interest in it. There is hardly a concert prospectus which does not feature a good

sprinkling of his works, and there is a plethora of recordings, at all price levels. Symphony No. 1, the 'Titan' is a splendid introduction to Mahler, with its pastoral first movement: 'Spring without end' as Mahler described it, plus a lively *Ländler* and a funeral march. Although this is a purely instrumental work, song tunes abound, some from an earlier cycle *Songs of a Wayfarer*, others familiar but in unexpected surroundings – 'Frère Jacques' is turned into a funeral march. Inside this funeral march there is an enigma, in the shape of a melody that has been identified by some (such as American composer/conductor Leonard Bernstein) as a Jewish lament. Mahler was Jewish, although he converted to the Roman Catholic faith, at least partly for reasons of career enhancement. The prestigious world of the Vienna Opera and Philharmonic Orchestra was thereby opened to him.

The Jewishness of this melody has been denied by some critics, who take the view that Mahler was a Viennese composer through and through, despite his ethnic origins. The only evidence we have is that of our ears, so you might like to listen to the piece and make up your own mind. It is in the third movement, and the tune appears after the altered (minor key) version of 'Frère Jacques'. This is just a small detail and not very important in itself, but it might just add further interest to an already enjoyable work. Personally, I always hear that particular section as an ethnic thumbprint of Mahler's, and, as much of his music can be thought of as autobiographical, it is perfectly logical that his first symphony should contain a brief reference to the composer's roots.

Strauss

The era of German Romanticism came to a close with Richard Strauss (1864–1949), whose symphonic poems we have encountered already (see Chapter 6). There are also 15 operas covering the opposite dramatic poles from the extremes of tragedy to comedy. In two successive operas we move from the Greek tragedy of *Electra* (1909) to *Der Rosenkavalier* (1911) which is as light as its predecessor is dark. Although Strauss took Wagnerian romanticism to its limit, towards the end of his life he returned to more traditional Classical–Romantic forms. The Oboe Concerto (1946), and the Duet-Concertino for Clarinet and Bassoon (1948), for example, display a degree of nostalgia for the Classical forms of Haydn and Mozart.

The orchestra of the late Romantics

Composers like Bruckner, Mahler and Strauss demanded a much larger orchestra than their predecessors. Here is the instrumentation required for Strauss's *Ein Heldenleben*:

Woodwind
piccolo, 3 flutes, 3 oboes, cor anglais, E flat clarinet, 2 B flat clarinets, bass clarinet, 3 bassoons, double bassoon.

Brass
5 trumpets, 3 trombones, 8 horns, tenor tuba, bass tuba*.

Percussion
timpani, bass drum, cymbals, tenor drum, side drum (or snare drum: a shallow, double-headed drum, with strips of wire or snares stretched against the lower head. These vibrate when the drum is struck, giving a characteristic 'crisp' response).

Strings
16 first violins, 16 second violins, 12 violas, 12 cellos, 8 double-basses, 2 harps.

*There is a group of instruments called 'Wagner tubas', which were originally prescribed by that composer for parts of *The Ring*, and by Bruckner in his last three symphonies. Wagner tubas look and sound like large members of the French horn family and are usually played by horn players.

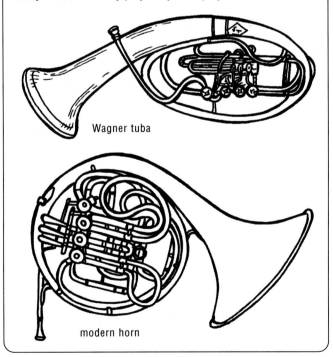

Wagner tuba

modern horn

During the years of Nazi domination, Strauss chose to remain in Germany (as did conductors Furtwängler and Karajan), a decision for which he was severely criticised after the war. He was never a party member, and did work with a Jewish librettist, but for many, by remaining he became indelibly associated with the Third Reich. The post-war *Metamorphosen* (1945), for 23 solo strings, which reworks part of the theme of the 'Eroica' Funeral March, has been seen variously as an elegy for Hitler, Strauss himself, and for a war-ravaged Germany. Performances of the piece were proscribed in Holland for a while, and when the Israel Philharmonic Orchestra was formed, all the music of Strauss and Wagner was excluded from their repertoire. Nowadays, the works of Strauss are evaluated on purely musical terms. The *Four Last Songs* (1948) are an evocative farewell to life from a tired and depressed artist, who had lived to see his beloved country destroyed by the obscenity of Nazism and the inevitable war that came in its wake.

Russia

We have seen in the preceding chapters how the influence of Austro-German culture was all pervading, particularly in the field of instrumental music. In the same way, Italian operatic styles had prevailed in most countries. During the nineteenth century, separate national identities gradually began to emerge. The Russians, for example, had long been subject to what is now called (in modern Australian parlance) the 'cultural cringe', characterized by a lack of regard for the culture of one's own country, coupled with an exaggerated valuation of foreign tastes, which are always assumed to be superior. Sophisticated Russians insisted on speaking French, the language of 'polite' society, and European imports were considered to be in every way preferable to the domestic products. Budding operatic composers were sent off to Italy to learn how to write in the Italian style.

Glinka and the Mighty Handful

Mikhail Glinka (1804–57) became known as 'The Father of Russian Music', in recognition of his efforts to restore the cultural self-esteem of the nation. He took Russian themes for his operas like *A Life for the Tsar*, and *Russlan and Ludmilla*, the latter being based on a poem by Pushkin, who was equally aware of the need for a national literature. Glinka also applied his Nationalist criteria to instrumental music in works like

Kamarinskya, which is based on Russian folk-tunes. This was the distinguishing feature of Russian musical nationalism, the melodies and rhythms of folk music providing the stamp of national identity. The example of Glinka inspired a new movement in Russian music that was carried forward by a group of composers who became known as 'The Five' or 'The Mighty Handful'. In order of seniority, they were: Alexander Borodin (1833–87), César Cui (1835–1918), Mily Balakirev (1837–1910), Modeste Mussorgsky (1839–81) and Nikolai Rimsky-Korsakov (1844–1908). They were not all composers by profession; Borodin, for example, was a professor of chemistry at the Academy of Medicine, St Petersburg, who found the time to produce two each of symphonies, string quartets and operas, all of which contained memorable melodies, drawn from folk sources. Best known is probably the opera *Prince Igor*, completed after his death by Rimsky-Korsakov and his pupil Glazunov, which included the famous *Polovtsian Dances*.

Cui was an army engineer who also wrote operas, and Mussorgsky, arguably the greatest of 'The Five', also embarked on a military career, later becoming a civil servant, until alcoholism took over. He was able, however, to complete the opera *Boris Godunov* (again, after Pushkin), a powerful and compelling work. Unfortunately, this was revised by Rimsky-Korsakov, who applied his academic training to smooth off some of the 'rough edges' in Mussorgsky's score, thereby depriving it of much of its sparkle and originality. More recent productions have reverted to the original score, restoring the composer's own unique orchestral colours. Balakirev was the musical mentor of 'The Five', a gifted teacher and composer with whom Rimsky-Korsakov studied, and absorbed his ideas of nationalism. The music of Wagner also influenced Rimsky-Korsakov, particularly in the field of orchestration, at which he became a master. Six operas form the bulk of his work, culminating in *The Golden Cockerel*, another Pushkin-inspired piece, which was at first banned from performance because it contained anti-government satire. Rimsky was dismissed from the St Petersburg Conservatory in 1905 for displaying revolutionary sympathies, but the authorities later relented and allowed him to return to his post. One of his pupils was Stravinsky, who was to turn the musical establishment upside down in a few years with *The Rite of Spring* (see Chapter 7), ensuring that the Russian musical tradition was continued into the twentieth century. In his instrumental music, Rimsky-Korsakov sometimes displayed a taste for the exotic, evident in the sunny *Capriccio Espagnol*, and the glittering *Scheherazade*, which display his orchestral mastery to the full.

Tchaikovsky

The best-known Russian composer of the nineteenth century, Peter Ilyich Tchaikovsky (1840–93) remained outside the activities of 'The Mighty Handful', maintaining a cordial but cool relationship with them. He was not averse to using folk melodies, as in the first string quartet and Symphony No. 2, but his works were never self-consciously Russian in character. In orchestral terms, Tchaikovsky's major achievement was in his mastery of the symphonic form, without direct reference to the German tradition in either its Brahmsian or Wagnerian manifestations. The six symphonies, plus the unnumbered programme symphony, *Manfred* (based on a story by Byron), demonstrate an imaginative use of the orchestra always expressive and utilizing its full dramatic potential, the broad sweep of the melodies stopping just short of the sentimental. Symphony No. 6, 'Pathetique' (1893), is particularly effective in the final slow movement, a bold innovation, coming after an affirmative march movement. The heartrending sadness of this closing theme presages Tchaikovsky's death just nine days after he conducted its first performance in St Petersburg. Much has been written on the tragedy of Tchaikovsky's personal life; his repressed homosexuality, suicide attempt, and the mysterious circumstances of his death. He drank a glass of unboiled water during a cholera epidemic in St Petersburg, contracted the disease, and died a few days later. Whether this was a deliberate act or not has been the subject of some speculation, and you might like to read one of the several biographies of the composer currently in print.

Eastern Europe and Scandinavia

Smetana

An authentic Bohemian style grew up during the nineteenth century, nurtured by the work of Bedřich Smetana (1824–84), who is known today for the set of six symphonic poems *Má Vlast* (My Country) which includes the popular melody in *Vltava* (a musical picture of the great river that flows through the city of Prague), and the folk-opera *The Bartered Bride*. The moving

String Quartet No. 1, 'From my Life', graphically portrays the onset of tinnitus, which was the precursor of the deafness which overcame him in his fiftieth year.

Dvořák

Smetana, Brahms and Wagner, were all formative influences on Antonin Dvořák (1841–1904), who was undoubtedly the most popular Czech composer outside his own country. Although he was prolific in all areas of composition, Dvořák's orchestral and chamber works are most familiar to audiences in the West. The final symphony, No. 9, 'From the New World' is a product of the composer's time spent in the USA, as director of the National Conservatory of Music, in New York (1892–5). The symphony is packed with familiar melodies, though many of them owe more to the Czech homeland than to the country of their dedication. The Cello Concerto of 1895 is another concert and recording favourite, and the Violin Concerto (1890) is frequently performed. The Czech musical tradition has continued through the work of composers like Leoš Janáček (1854–1928) and Bohuslav Martinů (1890–1959).

Grieg

A national awareness was also spreading across Scandinavia. Edvard Grieg (1843–1907), a Norwegian of Scottish descent, earned immortality for his incidental music for Ibsen's *Peer Gynt*, and provided generations of concert pianists with a splendid showpiece in his Piano Concerto in A minor. There are also many smaller-scale pieces for piano, based on folk-songs and dances.

Sibelius

A Finnish national music was forged by Jean Sibelius (1865–1957), through tone-poems, like the much-loved *Finlandia*, and symphonies of great individuality and conciseness of thought. In the final symphony, No. 7, all the material is presented and developed in a single ingeniously constructed movement. Sibelius received recognition from the Finnish government in the form of an annuity which enabled him to compose without the fear of financial problems. English composers like Vaughan Williams were particularly interested in Sibelius's music, seeing in it an alternative way of thinking to the Teutonic influences of Wagner and Brahms. There has always been a warmly appreciative audience for the music of Sibelius in the United Kingdom,

and there is no shortage of recordings. The Violin Concerto is a particularly effective and exciting piece which would make a good introduction to his work.

Nielsen

Carl Nielsen (1865–1931) was primarily a symphonist who shared with Sibelius a desire to move away from Wagnerian concepts. Instead, they envisaged a music less clouded by chromaticism and free from literary allusions. The symphony provided the best framework to achieve these aims and both composers took advantage of its flexibility. Nielsen composed six symphonies, of which No. 4, the 'Inextinguishable', with its large-scale finale is perhaps the best known. Symphony No. 5 (1922) is one of the most original and dramatic, bringing in the snare drum as a solo instrument, to represent the destructive element of war. The drummer is instructed to improvise 'as if at all costs he wants to impede the progress of the orchestra', which has embarked upon a triumphal theme. At the end of this first movement a lone clarinet mourns the destruction and the emptiness that it has left in its wake. The second movement finale is a brisk post-war call to order and brings the work to an optimistic close. The substance and content of Nielsen's work are now belatedly recognized, and performances outside his native Denmark are not as rare as they once were.

England

Elgar

After the massive influence of Handel, English music languished for a long time without producing composers of any great innovatory spirit. A number of Romantic composers visited its shores (Mendelssohn was on friendly terms with the royal family) but home-grown talent was thin on the ground. Towards the end of the nineteenth century, a batch of new composers including Hubert Parry (1848–1918), Charles Villiers Stanford (1852–1924, Irish-born, but worked in England) and Edward Elgar (1857–1934) arrived on the scene. In Elgar, English music found a Romantic voice of international quality. He lacked the academic training of Parry and Stanford, and despite this (or because of it), surpassed them in inventiveness. Elgar's father owned a music shop in Worcester, and young Edward studied the scores he found there. He became involved in every aspect of local musical life as violinist, bassoonist, organist and conductor.

Elgar's style of composition was not derived from any single musical tradition, nor was he a nationalist, in the sense of making use of folk sources. Nevertheless, there is something intrinsically English about much of his work, and jingoistic elements have been attached to some, like the *Pomp and Circumstance Marches*, which are an inevitable part of the Last Night of the Proms excesses. But the two symphonies, the oratorio *The Dream of Gerontius*, and the concertos for violin and cello are works of undisputed quality, as is the set of variations of 1899, 'on an original theme for orchestra', subtitled *Enigma*. Each of the 14 variations is a character sketch of an individual, including Elgar himself, his wife and their friends. The 'enigma' is said to refer not to the identity of the subjects (given in the score by initials, nicknames or merely asterisks), but to a hidden theme, which is thought by some to be 'Auld Lang Syne'.

The Cello Concerto is a marvellously passionate work, which has been described 'un-English' in its emotional intensity. The interpretation by the cellist Jacqueline du Pré, with the London Symphony Orchestra conducted by John Barbirolli in 1965, has never been bettered. Elgar lived to see the age of recording, and supervised the young Yehudi Menuhin in a recorded performance of his violin concerto. His works continue to be popular in the United Kingdom but are not well known in Europe or America. Visiting British orchestras perform them all over the world, however, with great success.

Delius

Some English composers did take an interest in folk music and based orchestral works upon it, as did Frederick Delius (1862–1934) in *Brigg Fair*, a large orchestral piece subtitled *An English Rhapsody*, which subjected a folk-tune (collected by Percy Grainger) to 17 variations, with linking passages and a coda. Delius was a cosmopolitan character, born of German parents in Bradford, equally at home in Germany, France and America. Most of his compositions were examples of Impressionistic tone painting, though there is some early chamber music. Towards the end of his life, though blind and paralysed, Delius continued to compose, with the help of an amanuensis, a fellow Yorkshireman, the late Eric Fenby, whose book *Delius as I knew him*, makes fascinating reading.

We came across *On Hearing the First Cuckoo in Spring* in Chapter 05, and you might like to use this piece as a test to see whether you like Delius's music. If so, there are four operas, three concertos and several choral works to try.

Vaughan Williams

'The English school of composition will not be founded on English folk-song', may seem a surprising remark from Ralph Vaughan Williams (1872–1958), who was a prominent member of the English Folk Song Society, since 1904, soon after its inception. He wrote and lectured widely on the place of national character in music, but he had in mind a more general idea of 'roots', than the mere grafting of a folk melody on to an alien superstructure for the sake of instant identity. Without being chauvinistic, Vaughan Williams wished to foster the growth of a national music that was not indebted to foreign models, particularly the Austro-German brand of late Romanticism.

Unlike Elgar, Vaughan Williams received a conventional academic musical training at the Royal College of Music and Cambridge University. He also studied in Berlin and Paris under Max Bruch and Ravel, which may have mitigated the conservatism of his earlier studies. He edited the English Hymnal in 1906 and during his long career covered most types of musical composition, including, as we have already noted (in Chapter 07) film music. His nine symphonies (that significant number again) encompass remarkably different moods and styles. The first two, the 'Sea' and 'London', are strongly pictorial, while the third or 'Pastoral' is much more than the mere evocation of the countryside that some contemporary critics took it to be (one 'wit' said it was 'like a cow looking over a gate'). In fact it is a moving memorial to those young men who were killed in the First World War, one of whom was George Butterworth, a personal friend of Vaughan Williams, fellow folk-song enthusiast and composer. The tragedy of young lives cut short is underlined by wistful solos for horn and trumpet in the second movement.

Symphony No. 4, in contrast, is a conscious attempt to tackle a more modern idiom, with violent dissonances and aggressive orchestration shot through with two simple four-note themes. The jagged rhythms were thought by some to mirror Williams's irascible nature. His own, much-quoted comment about the work was typical: 'I don't know whether I like it, but it's what I meant'. Some of the orchestral works have become popular favourites, like his *Fantasia on a theme by Thomas Tallis* (1910). An aspect of folk-song that particularly appealed to Vaughan Williams was its modal character, operating outside the 'normal' major/minor harmonic scheme, and this was also true of some pieces by Thomas Tallis (1505–85) that he discovered while working on the English Hymnal. The orchestral fantasia based on one of the tunes has a haunting, timeless quality which has played its part in the revival of interest in the Elizabethan composers by twentieth-century audiences.

Holst

Early interests in folk music led to pieces like *Somerset Rhapsody* and *Cotswolds Symphony*, but Gustav Holst (1874–1934) also looked further afield for inspiration, occasionally venturing outside the European musical tradition to the East. He experimented with Indian music and literature in *Hymns from the Rig-Veda*, and the chamber opera *Savitri*. Holst composed operas, choral music and songs (in between his teaching duties at St Paul's Girls' School in London), but one work stands out in the public consciousness above all others, and that is the orchestral **suite** *The Planets*. Holst's only excursion into large-scale orchestral territory demands Straussian resources, including organ and female chorus. Each movement represents a planet, and the character ascribed to it, beginning with 'Mars, the Bringer of War'. It is significant that Holst began to sketch this movement in 1914, as Europe was about to hurl itself into a terrible conflict. The thundering **ostinato** (repeated) rhythms, and the heavy artillery of brass and percussion spell out the approaching threat in unequivocal terms. The contrasting 'Venus, the Bringer of Peace', is a quiet contemplative movement with solo violin, cello and oboe.

'Neptune, the Mystic' is the final planet to be visited, and here Holst takes us into the other musical worlds, reminiscent of the Impressionism of Ravel and Debussy (see Chapter 05). Two alternating chords, gently floating on a wordless cloud of soft voices, create an atmosphere of other-wordliness. Instruments like the harp and celeste (a small keyboard instrument producing a metallic, tinkling tone) add to the mysterious, ethereal effect. Appropriately, the first performance of this music was given in London in 1918, at the end of the First World War. This was a time for contemplation of humanity, civilisation, and, in Holst's case, spirituality. Elsewhere in Europe, radical changes were taking place alongside the last vestiges of Romanticism.

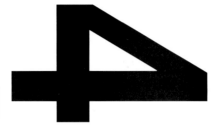

modernism and beyond

In this chapter you will learn:

- about the restless and continuous changes of the twentieth century, and examine some of the ways in which composers have experimented with new and radical ideas

- about the development of some revolutionary modernist methods such as atonality, serialism and electronics, going on to cover jazz and minimalism. The chapter closes with a selection of contemporary composers.

Chromaticism

The delicate washes of orchestral colour that we enjoyed from Debussy in Chapter 05 also had the effect of loosening the strict relationship between harmony, form and especially key that had informed the symphonic writing of earlier composers. The normal or **diatonic** system of scales, with chords built on each note of the scale, was expanded by using the smaller **intervals** (called **chromatic**, which means 'colourful') between the steps of the scale. Debussy literally filled in the spaces between the notes with colour, consequently weakening the pull of the tonal, or 'key' centre. In works like the *Prélude à l'après-midi d'un faune* and the ballet *Jeux* there is a harmonic vagueness and a lack of the forward momentum we tend to expect from more conventional symphonic music.

Schoenberg

Chromaticism was also explored by Wagner, famously in *Tristan and Isolde,* whose opening chords do not resolve in the conventional way, leaving the listener unsure of the key. Mahler and Strauss followed this lead and indulged in a little tonal ambiguity of their own, but they did not

Schoenberg

go so far as to abandon the concept of key altogether. This particular nettle was grasped by Arnold Schoenberg (or Schönberg, 1874–1951), a composer who was very firmly part of the Austro-German tradition (his early works are in the Romantic post Wagnerian mould), who consciously strove to extend that tradition by taking what he saw as the next logical step into complete chromaticism, removing any notion of a tonal centre. Up until this time music had always been controlled by a root note which provided an anchor, a starting and finishing point, to the work. This is true not only of music from the period of tonality, when major and minor keys became the norm, roughly from Bach onwards, but also of earlier music, when other types of scales or modes were employed. The key-based system of harmony had not yet been devised, but there was always a fundamental controlling note to provide the ear with a point of reference.

Atonality

Schoenberg's idea was to remove this hierarchical system of tonality and treat all the 12 notes within any given scale (including all the sharps and flats) as equal. Early works composed according to this new theory include *Erwartung* (Expectation), completed in 1909 (though not performed until 1924), an opera for a single character, a woman, who wanders through a forest in search of her lover, eventually to discover his murdered body. Schoenberg worked quickly on this piece, in a fury of inspiration, always aware of the radical nature of what he was doing. He compared his feelings at this time to having fallen into a boiling sea, and trying to swim against the current. A talented amateur painter, Schoenberg was identified with the German Expressionists, whose work was characterized by bold use of colour and subject matter which reflected frank psychological insight into subconscious emotions (Sigmund Freud was an influential figure in Vienna at the time).

In the Five Orchestral Pieces, Op. 16, composed in the same year as *Erwartung*, there is tone painting of the purest kind. Schoenberg described the work as 'without architecture, without structure; only an ever changing unbroken succession of colours, rhythms and moods'. The intensity of these colours is varied by the dynamics and changes in instrumental texture. There were some attempts to add extra musical imagery to the pieces, for

example, the third is said to represent the morning sun playing upon the surface of a lake, but the composer's title for this section was simply 'chord colours'. What we don't get from this music is a tune to hold on to – there is no theme to be developed. The old sonata-form certainties are gone, so we need to adopt a new listening strategy. We must concentrate instead on the elements that are present: colours made up of the entire musical spectrum, modified by instrumental sounds, rhythm and dynamics. This is the musical equivalent of an abstract painting. The art of Schoenberg's construction conceals itself to produce music that transcends all the previous conventions and becomes something new. It is paradoxical, though, that this tightly controlled music sounds random and unorganised, but the composer was keen that the methods of organization should not be discernible to the ear.

Berg and Webern

Schoenberg was a gifted and charismatic teacher, and, although he did not proselytize, he attracted some exceptional pupils, including Alban Berg (1885–1935) and Anton Webern (1883–1945), who were fascinated by the notions of **atonality**. With their teacher, they became known as the 'Second Viennese School', all working with the new **'twelve-note'** system, as it became known ('twelve-tone' in the United States), but moving in different directions. Berg's work was perhaps the most accessible with operas *Wozzeck* and *Lulu* and the Violin Concerto, in which he managed to introduce tonal elements to mitigate the severity of the music.

Webern's music is more austere, with a stricter application of twelve-note techniques, but he had the good sense to realize that such intensely wrought music would lose its effect if he attempted to extend it too far. He therefore made his musical statements with great brevity and conciseness. Everything he had to say was compressed into the smallest possible space, in fact he confessed that once all the 12 notes had been stated, he felt that there was little else to say. In the sets of orchestral pieces composed between 1909 and 1913, hardly any last for more than one minute. The orchestral method used by Webern was *klangfarbenmelodie*, begun by Schoenberg in the Five Pieces, which refers to rapid changes of instrumentation, constantly altering the tone-colours of the 12-note line. The kaleidoscopic effect of this technique, combined with the density of the musical matter, requires great concentration on the part of the listener.

Serialism

Around 1921, Schoenberg formalized the means of structuring his atonal music, which he hoped would replace the tonal system, and provide a way forward for Austro-German music. The method was that the 12 notes would be laid out in a predetermined order or 'row', and always presented in the correct order, either horizontally (as melody) or vertically (as chords). It was also possible to play the series of notes backwards (retrograde form) and upside down (inverted form). Serialism, as this technique came to be known, was taken up and developed by a small, but influential, selection of composers across Europe and the United States. Olivier Messiaen (1908–92) and his pupils Pierre Boulez (b.1925) and Karlheinz Stockhausen (b.1928), were among those who envisaged an extension of Schoenberg's ideas towards a notion of 'total serialism'. Taking the mathematical purity of Webern's music as their model, they set about applying serial methodology to all the components of musical organization, including rhythm and even dynamics. Such emphasis on mathematical control logically led to the use of computers and synthesizers, when they became available.

Inevitably, the more complex the music became, the less immediate was the appeal for the listener. Serialist music was often perceived as dry, severely academic and cerebral, created for and appealing to an intellectual elite. The fact remains that the music of the Second Viennese School, almost a century after it was written, is still thought of as 'difficult' by many listeners. Their 12-note compositions have never become staple orchestral concert items, despite a universal acknowledgement of their originality, sincerity and musical mastery. It is true to say that some of Beethoven's and Mozart's music was also considered difficult in its time, but it did not take all that long for audiences to catch up, and their works soon came to be fully appreciated and frequently performed.

Problems with atonality

Should we, then, think the unthinkable, that the 12-note experiment was a mistake, an interesting exercise in pushing chromaticism to its extreme, but in the process losing touch with its audience? Perhaps Schoenberg's own misgivings were well founded. He once referred to the effect of his early atonal compositions as 'nightmare', in response to hostile criticism. Schoenberg was sensitive enough to appreciate the difficulties his new works would cause to ears accustomed to tonal music. Recent research has shown that there is a negative reaction in the brain when notes that are not tonally related are played, either together or consecutively. Critics of atonality would say we respond positively to tonal music because there is a natural system of harmony, which exists whenever a note is sounded. A series of related pitches is set in motion, not always immediately audible, but when separated out and put together produce an agreeable or harmonious sound. The higher harmonies are more remote, but the basic note is the well-spring from which the whole series is created. Combinations of notes from this series produce tonal harmony, always related to the fundamental or lowest note.

As we have seen in previous chapters, the whole system of tonal music is based on these harmonic series, with the steps of the major and minor scales constructed from them, and separate chords built on each step of the scales. The excitement is generated by a temporary movement away from the fundamental or key-note, and satisfaction obtained by the eventual return to it. Schoenberg was aware of the cataclysmic effect on the ear or removing the key-centre, but his intellectual curiosity forced him to pursue the logical course of musical development as he saw it. By denying what now seems to be a physical need for a tonal foundation (and therefore a hierarchical system of musical organization), he was indeed swimming against the tide.

It is possible for the human intellect to perceive and understand abstract artworks of various kinds, and there can be satisfaction in unravelling a complex puzzle, or

The synthesizer

The synthesizer is an electronic instrument capable of producing and reproducing an enormous variety of sounds. It can mimic conventional instruments, or supply any combination of pitches, timbres and rhythms that the player cares to select. The American composer Milton Babbitt used an early synthesizer developed by RCA in a serial work *Ensembles for Synthesizer* (1962–4). The instrument used by Babbitt was fairly primitive by modern standards, making use of punched paper tape, but a more compact synthesizer first developed by Robert Moog, has since been taken up by all kinds of musicians from the rock, pop and film-music worlds to the avant-garde, especially the more mathematically-inclined composers like Stockhausen and Iannis Xenakis (b.1922), who are interested in computer-generated sounds.

going against the grain of normal practices, but this type of intellectual gratification is not the only thing that people seek from a musical performance. There is a real danger of producing music for an intellectual elite which excludes a large potential audience. The serialist's rationale is that the tonal system was only a phase in the history of musical development, and, at the beginning of the twentieth century, it was becoming stale. Serialism can then be seen as merely a new way of ordering musical sounds. But it must be remembered that a fundamental hierarchy of musical organization had existed long before the major and minor scales were ever devised. The medieval modes, for example, were always dependent upon the 'final', or fundamental note on which the mode was founded and to which it always returned. There was also a 'dominant' note, five steps higher than the final, as there is in the tonal system. We must not underestimate the enormity of the break with all previous musical practices that serialism represents.

Stravinsky and serialism

Some composers have shown that it is possible to employ 12-note methods as part of a more eclectic approach. In his later works, Schoenberg tempered his use of 12-note rows to admit some semblance of harmony, which earlier atonal practices would not have allowed. A surprisingly late convert to serialism was Stravinsky who had always welcomed new forms of musical discipline, and he sought alternatives and additions to the conventions of tonal harmony, whether in the pounding rhythms of *The Rite of Spring*, or in his adaptations of early contrapuntal techniques of his so-called 'Neoclassical' (more accurately neo-Baroque) period. However, his music always retained its personal characteristics, whatever constraints he placed upon himself. His final work, the *Requiem Canticles* (1965–6), was based on serial methods, after which he fell silent, owing to ill health, until his death in 1971. Like Mozart, he had written his own musical epitaph.

Different directions

To many musicians, serialism is just one of several techniques to be acquired, as part of their armoury of compositional skills. Other ideas might include experimentation with different scales and modes, **polytonality** (different keys employed simultaneously) and **microtonality** (the use of intervals smaller than a

semitone), as well as tonal forms (Stravinsky would often pointedly state a key in the titles of his works). Béla Bartók (1881–1945) used several of these methods, often adapted from the folk-songs of his native Hungary, of which he was an avid collector. Orchestral works like *Music for Strings, Percussion and Celesta* (1937), *Concerto for Orchestra* (1943), and the six string quartets contain music of great originality, without being connected to any particular discipline or 'school'.

Tuned percussion

Xylophone

Bartok's *Music for Strings, Percussion and Celesta* makes use of a range of percussion instruments including the xylophone, which consists of a set of wooden bars, set out in the same pattern as a keyboard, the longer, producing the lowest notes, to the left, diminishing in size towards the right. There may be a set of resonating tubes positioned beneath the bars to amplify the sound, but this is not always the case. The bars are struck with two or more round-headed mallets held by a single player, producing a distinctive bright sound.

Marimba

Equivalent instruments to the xylophone are found in most cultures, for example the marimba, an instrument of African origin, always widely used in Latin America, is now (thanks to modern composers and enlightened teachers) fairly common in Europe too. This instrument is very similar to the xylophone, but is slightly deeper in pitch and comes equipped with large resonating tubes. It is normally played with soft mallets, which, combined with the lower register of the instrument, produce a softer, mellower tone than the xylophone.

Glockenspiel

The glockenspiel looks like a small xylophone (without resonating tubes), except that the bars are made of metal. The sound produced when struck with wooden mallets is metallic and bell-like, akin to the celesta, but capable of a harder attack.

Vibraphone

The youngest member of this family is the vibraphone. It is a hybrid, with metal bars, but also a full set of resonating tubes. Beneath each bar, at the top of the tube, is a disc, which revolves when an electric motor is switched on, performing a dual function of sustaining the note and adding a controllable **vibrato**. A foot-operated damper enables the player to control the length of the note. Berg wrote an important part for the instrument in the opera *Lulu*, and Messiaen in the *Turangalîla Symphony* (see 'Nature and orientalism', pages 89–90). There have also been a number of virtuoso jazz vibraphonists, including Lionel Hampton, Milt Jackson and Gary Burton.

A significant number of twentieth-century composers managed to find new things to say through broadly tonal means. We have already noted some of the late Romantics, like Mahler, Strauss and Elgar, but later composers chose to use existing forms to produce what was essentially new music. Some, like the German Paul Hindemith (1895–1963), felt that music ought to be useful to society, and their work was dubbed *Gebrauchsmusik* (utility music). The anti-elitist sentiments implicit in this led to a good deal of music for amateur performance being written by Hindemith, as well as works for pianola and mechanical organ.

Britain – Britten, Walton and Tippett

In Britain, Benjamin Britten (1913–76) wrote for the GPO film unit for two years, before producing the great operas and choral works for which he is justly renowned. William Walton (1902–83) wrote film music, scoring a series of Shakespeare films for Laurence Olivier in addition to the renowned *Façade*, in which he set to music the poems of Edith Sitwell, and orchestral works including the beguiling Viola Concerto. The most eclectic and difficult to categorize of his generation of English composers is Michael Tippett (b.1905), who has shown the influence of many contemporary sources, and, like Britten, early English music. He was always sensitive to social and political injustice. His wartime oratorio *A Child of our Time* (1941, performed 1944) addresses the reality of Jewish persecution by the Nazis, and uses negro spirituals as Bach might have employed chorale tunes. Two decades later, Britten's *War Requiem* (written for the consecration of the new Coventry Cathedral, in 1962), based on the war poetry of Wilfred Owen, juxtaposed with the Latin Requiem Mass, presses home the point about the futility of war.

United States – Copland and Ives

A new phenomenon appeared in the twentieth century in the form of American nationalism, emanating from composers like Aaron Copland (1900–90), who introduced American themes and elements of Latin American music and jazz into compositions like *Appalachian Spring*, *El Salon Mexico* and *Quiet City*. Copland was always concerned with communicating with his audience, a trait that was not shared by his compatriot Charles Ives (1874–1954) who was older than Copland but more unorthodox in his musical ideas. Ives rejoiced in conflicting themes and keys, and traditional American tunes can be heard colliding, as though two marching bands had met unexpectedly, in pieces like *Three Places in New England* and *Washington's Birthday*. We shall return to the United States later in this chapter, to look at more recent developments.

The former Soviet Union – Shostakovich and Prokofiev

Working in Stalin's Russia, Sergei Prokofiev (1891–1953) and Dmitri Shostakovich (1906–75) were restricted in the amount of new ideas they could incorporate into their music. Experimentation was soon curtailed by the government, and any tendency towards modernism was condemned as counter-revolutionary formalism. Music should be simple, tuneful and optimistic, the Leader decreed, so that the workers could understand it. Soviet Realism took the idea of utility music to the extreme. It was the antithesis of the elitism of the serialist composers. After Shostakovich's opera *The Lady Macbeth of Mtensk* was denounced in *Pravda*, his next symphony, No. 5 (1937), was subtitled 'a Soviet artist's creative reply to just criticism'. It is hard not to see Symphony No. 5, with its mock-heroic tunes as ironic, and yet it has undoubted charms, and, given a straightforward reading, is a stirring work. Shostakovich went on to write another ten symphonies, including the moving 'Leningrad' (No. 7), composed during the siege of that city in 1941.

After the Russian Revolution, Prokofiev spent some time in Europe and America, returning, to his homeland in 1933, to encounter censure, but was regarded highly enough by 1951 to be awarded a Stalin prize. His music is always tuneful, although his early operas, whimsically titled *The Love for Three Oranges* and *The Nose*, have an ironic edge. The first symphony (of seven), the 'Classical' uses eighteenth-century forms, length and orchestra, but with the composer's individual melodic style. Prokofiev had imagined what sort of music Haydn might write if he were alive in the twentieth century. The ballet *Romeo and Juliet* has many deliciously Romantic features, and, as we saw in Chapter 07, Prokofiev also wrote some stirring film music, particularly for the director Eisenstein.

France – 'Les Six' and Erik Satie

In Paris, the writer and film director Jean Cocteau also acted as mentor to a group of composers who came to be known as *Les Six*. Cocteau's idea was that music should be modern, clear, elegant and, above all, French. The name was adapted from the Russian 'Five', but there was not the same interest in national music to hold them together. They collaborated on a couple of projects, including an album of piano pieces, but achieved more as individuals. Prominent members of 'Les Six' were Darius Milhaud (1892–1974), Francis Poulenc (1899–1963) and the Swiss-born Arthur Honegger (1892–1955). The group's associate (though never a member) was Erik Satie (1866–1925), who was the least orthodox and arguably the most inventive of all.

Satie's witty pieces came closest to Cocteau's ideal, mostly in the form of piano pieces (he had worked as a café pianist), but also three ballet scores, songs and choral works. An eccentric in life as in music, Satie was never confident of his composing technique, even after years of study at the Paris Conservatoire. He reacted to criticisms of his control of form by producing a series of 'pear-shaped' pieces. His harmony was unconventional as were the titles of his works, like *Five Grimaces*, *La belle exentrique* and *Sonatine bureaucratique* which need no translation. He was also way ahead of his time in writing 'furniture music', which was not intended to be listened to. How ironic that Satie's tongue-in-cheek idea should later be turned into a multinational business in the 'background' music industry.

Sounds of modern life

The Italian Futurists, a group of artists and poets, rejoiced in the products of the Machine Age. Cars, aeroplanes and factories were symbols of modern life that were to be glorified and made the subject of various kinds of artworks. Luigi Russolo (1885–1947), a painter, assembled huge loudspeaker-like devices to simulate electronically the sounds of everyday mechanical noises. The instruments were demonstrated in London and Paris before the First World War, and aroused the interest of some musicians, including Stravinsky (who seemed to have a finger in every twentieth-century pie), and Edgard Varése (1885–1965). Varése was interested in **timbre**, which roughly means 'quality of sound', and was, to him, as important a musical element as melody or harmony. He liked the immediacy of attack of wind and percussion instruments, but he also envisaged an electronic instrument which could produce a limitless range and variety of sounds and rhythms. He had, of course, foreseen the modern synthesizer, however, his imagination was way ahead of the technology of his time.

Early electronic instruments

Two instruments seem to have survived from the many experiments in the early years of the twentieth century. Both were invented in the 1920s, and both bear the name of their inventors.

Thérémin

The Thérémin, presented to the world by Léon Thérémin in 1920, produces a note when the hand is placed near to an upright rod, rather like a car aerial. The pitch is varied by raising or lowering the hand, which creates a sliding effect, from note to note. The instrument is not capable of playing chords or **staccato** (detached) passages. A few composers have written parts for the Thérémin, including Martinu, but it seems to have found a niche for itself in the film music and sound-effect field, often used to create 'spooky' effects in horror films.

Ondes Martinot

The ondes Martinot, patented in 1922 by Maurice Martinot, is assured of a permanent place in the modern orchestra, having been specified by Milhaud, Honegger, Varése, Messiaen and others. Volume and tone colour can be varied, and the instrument is usually (but not always) fitted with a keyboard.

Two *ondes Martinot* (see above) feature in Varése's *Ecuatorial* (1934), plus brass, piano, organ and chorus. It was not until the 1950s that he began to produce works for music on magnetic tape, like *Poème électronique*, which uses solo voice, percussion, electronic and natural sounds. The technique of manipulating recorded electronic sounds was pioneered by a Parisian musician and engineer, Pierre Schaeffer in 1948, and called *musique concrète*. Everyday sounds could be taken and altered, speeded up, slowed down or distorted according to the creative imagination of the controller. Purely electronic sounds could also be created, or conventional musical instruments could be recorded and subjected to electronic alteration. Stockhausen did a large amount of work using both live and recorded electronics. An interesting example of this is *Kontakte* (1961), which is a piece for a four-channel tape with optional parts for piano and percussion.

Nature and orientalism: new influences

In the history of Western music, the one basic element that has been underdeveloped is rhythm. Stravinsky redressed the balance to some extent with *The Rite of Spring*, but his relentless spirit soon moved on to new projects and innovations, though always with a strong rhythmic base. *The Rite* may have seemed strange and primitive to some, but the idea of using rhythmic sequences or 'cells' as a controlling feature of music had been planted in the minds of the more adventurous composers. Messiaen was always interested in rhythmic organization, and looked to the East for new methods. He adapted Indian rhythmic patterns and Balinese gamelan sounds (gongs and drums) in his more ambitious works. The massive, ten-movement *Turangalîla Symphony* (1948) has elements of these, plus birdsong, which the composer collected, notated and increasingly utilized in his works. The *ondes Martinot* played a prominent part in this work, added an exotic sound, along with the vibraphone and glockenspiel, which suggest the effect of Balinese gongs.

Cage

Another remarkable artist who took an interest in Eastern music was John Cage (1912–92). While Messiaen concerned himself only with musical forms and remained a devout Roman Catholic, Cage embraced philosophical ideas of the Orient like Zen Buddhism and the *I Ching*, which influenced his compositions. Many of his early works were for percussion ensembles, until he devised the 'prepared piano', which was a method of exploiting the percussive possibilities of the piano, by wedging a variety of objects between the strings of the instrument, altering its sound to emphasize the rhythmic aspect of the music he wrote for it. Cage also experimented with **aleatoric** methods, which introduced random or 'chance' elements into the music. In one composition for piano, *Music of Changes* (1951), the player tosses a coin to determine details of the performance. The most notorious Cage composition is undoubtedly *4′33″* (1952), nominally written for piano, the piece consists of 4 minutes and 33 seconds of silence, or at least the player is not instructed to touch the keyboard during that time. For Cage, the music exists in whatever sounds might happen in the room, all the inevitable noises that occur at any musical performance: coughing, rustling, scraping of chairs, and so on, plus any external sounds which may be audible from inside the building. Obviously, every performance would be unique and unrepeatable. Electronic music also held great fascination for Cage, and he applied aleatoric ideas to it. One device, used in *Radio Music* and *Imaginary Landscapes* (1951) was to assemble a number of radios and have operators alter the channels, constantly changing the sound mix. Stockhausen later used shortwave radios in *Kurzwellen* ('Shortwaves', 1968) alongside other instruments. He and Boulez both experimented with chance techniques in their compositions.

Minimalism

In the late 1960s, a few musicians in the United States wanted to create a music which was more accessible than the dense intellectual products of the European aftermath of the Second Viennese School. They were interested in rhythm, as Cage had been, and studied Indian and African music, admiring both the lack of emphasis on harmony, and the rhythmic sophistication. A small melodic or rhythmic motif could be extended into a large work by means of repetition, harmonic stasis and gradual metamorphosis. Steve Reich (b.1936) found a verbal expression of his guiding principle in the phrase 'How small a thought it takes to fill a whole life'. The American **minimalists**, as they came to be called, were aware of the repeated bass lines and pared-down harmonic sequences that were a feature of much rock, soul music, and jazz (particularly of John Coltrane) in the 1960s and 1970s, so they were able to communicate with a larger audience than most modern composers could expect.

Early minimalist experiments concentrated on tape loops, taking a fragment of music, or a speech pattern, as Reich did with a black pentacostal preacher in 'It's Gon' Rain', repeating it to emphasize the musicality of the speech. Reich became fascinated by canonic forms (see Chapter 09), as in *Clapping Music* (1972), when two players begin by clapping a short rhythmic pattern in unison. When one player drops a beat, the two parts are sent out of phase, setting off a whole series of new rhythmic patterns, until eventually the two parts return to unison, when the piece ends. Similar techniques were used in *Piano Phase*, *Violin Phase* and *Drumming* (1971), this last being inspired by the rhythmic counterpoint of West African musicians. The setting of words prompts a more melodic response from the minimalists. Philip Glass (b.1937) and John Adams (b.1947) have produced successful operas, in broadly minimalist form, such as Glass's *Akhnaten* (1984) and Adams's *Nixon in China* (1987). In Europe, Stockhausen (his name recurs in the second half of the century as much as Stravinsky's does in the first) in works like *Stimmung* (1968), based on the harmonic series, and *Mantra* (1970) for two electronically modulated pianos, exploits the idea of repetition and harmonic stasis in ways not related to the American model. However, the word 'minimalism' is now associated with the works of Americans like Terry Riley, Philip Glass, Steve Reich and John Adams, with the addition of some British followers, such as Michael Nyman (see Chapter 07).

Minimalism has been criticized from within the musical establishment. Julliard School of Music graduates Reich and Glass worked as New York taxi drivers before their work was accepted, first by the art world. Condemned by the musical cognoscenti as purveyors of mindless repetition, their earliest concerts were in art galleries rather than concert halls. Their critics failed to perceive the subtle changes that went on within the music. When listening to minimalist music, there is no point in listening for things which will not be there. There will be little harmonic movement, no development section, but there will be a development of a new kind, a very gradual change. There is tonality in abundance, the music never changes key and there is rhythmic variation which is often very complex. If you enjoy rhythmic patterns, and can adjust your mind to a slow pace of harmonic change, minimalism can provide an experience every bit as satisfying as any other type of music. Experiment with a short piece, such as Philip Glass's *Façade* for two soprano saxophones and string orchestra, Steve Reich's *Clapping Music* or John Adams's *Short Ride in a Fast Machine*.

Jazz

The interest of the minimalists in non-European music and rhythmic importance leads us to the most exciting new form of music to emerge in the twentieth century. Unfortunately, there is not space here to give a detailed history of the music which had been fermenting and developing throughout the century as a unique fusion of African and European musical strengths. Jazz has proved to be one of the most powerful and artistically viable musics of the twentieth century. When so many European composers seemed to be painting themselves into an intellectual corner, there emerged a bright, vibrant form which breathed life into the weary conventions of European harmonic thought. There has been a lot of patronizing nonsense written about the influence of jazz on European music. Many composers have toyed with a few jazz-like figures in their essentially European compositions, like Debussy, Hindemith, Weill, Poulenc, Copland, Gershwin and Bernstein. In 1945, Stravinsky dedicated his *Ebony Concerto* to jazz clarinetist and bandleader Woody Herman, who gave the first performance of this interesting piece which turned out to be more Stravinsky than jazz.

The essential elements of jazz are rhythm (remember Ellington: 'It don't mean a thing if it ain't got that swing') and improvization, a practice that has disappeared from European music since the age of Bach and Handel. The really great jazz artists have been supreme improvisers, like Louis Armstrong, Charlie Parker, Miles Davis and John Coltrane, musicians who could weave an endless garment of pure gold from the most unpromising cloth, but there have also been composers of genius, like Duke Ellington, Thelonius Monk and Charles Mingus. The point is that jazz is not merely a folk-source that 'serious' composers can tap into to add spice and urban atmosphere to their works when they feel like it. It is a serious and viable form in its own right, one of the few with any vitality and potential for the future. Happily, the barriers between different musical cultures are now breaking down. Musicians like the trumpet player Wynton Marsalis, who has already made his reputation as a soloist in the worlds of both classical music and jazz, have chosen to specialize in jazz. Marsalis is both a composer and a performer. Jazz has spread to Europe with musicians like Jan Gabarek of Norway and John Surman of the United Kingdom producing a specifically European version of the music. American and European jazz goes from strength to strength with new talent appearing all the time, and at the beginning of the twentieth-first century the future looks healthy.

The saxophone

This fascinating hybrid was invented by Adolphe Sax in 1846. Although it is made of brass, it is blown and fingered as a woodwind instrument, with a single reed housed in a clarinet-like mouthpiece. Sax may have intended it as a military band instrument, as it is capable of considerable volume of sound. Symphonic composers were initially slow to adopt the saxophone, but it has been given prominent parts in works by Strauss, Ravel, Bizet, Vaughan Williams, Prokofiev and Stravinsky, among others, and solo works have been written by Debussy, Glasunov, Hindemith and Philip Glass. The instrument is available in several different sizes, the most common being the soprano (usually, but not always, straight), plus alto, tenor and baritone, all in the familiar curved shape. There are also sopranino, bass, and 'C melody' (between the alto and tenor in pitch) versions, but these are rarely seen.

In the symphonic context, saxophones are often found singly or in pairs. Strauss calls for four in his *Sinfonia Domestica*, and Ravel three in *Bolero* (sopranino, soprano and alto). There is an increasing volume of repertoire for the saxophone quartet, comprising the four most common sizes, and in jazz, the normal 'big band' sax section is made up of two altos, two tenors and baritone, though there is frequent variation of this formula by the musicians 'doubling' more than one size of instrument as well as other woodwinds like the flute and clarinet.

Played 'straight' as a solo instrument, the saxophone can sound rather bland, but its unique quality is its ability to alter its sound according to the individual characteristics of the player. This amazing versatility has been exploited to the full by jazz musicians, who each have an individual sound on the instrument. For example, Charlie Parker, Art Pepper, Cannonball Adderley and Ornette Coleman all produced utterly different and instantly recognizable sounds from the alto, while Coleman Hawkins, Lester Young, Stan Getz and John Coltrane all had their own inimitable sounds on the tenor. Duke Ellington recognized this phenomenon and wrote his orchestral parts for people rather than instruments. To some extent, all jazz musicians have their own sound, whatever the instrument, but the saxophone produces a tabula rasa, on which the improvising musician can write his or her own personality.

saxophone

Further listening

A gallimaufry of 20th century composers

This chapter has provided a broad outline of the various styles and movements in twentieth-century music. There are inevitably many worthwhile composers who have not yet been mentioned and whose music you may want to investigate. Here is short, and far from comprehensive list, with brief descriptions of their individual styles.

Samuel Barber (1910–81)

Barber was an American composer who was never seduced by the atonal revolution that swept over from Europe and maintained a stranglehold on modern music for much of the twentieth century. He has been regarded as a 'one work' composer, because his Adagio for Strings (an arrangement of the second movement of his String Quartet) received a disproportionate amount of public attention. However, his violin concerto (1940) has also proved an enduring piece and found a place in the mainstream concert repertoire. There are also three symphonies, cello and piano concertos, and two operas, making a small but significant body of work, which has survived into the twenty-first century.

Elliott Carter (1908–95)

Several American composers rose to prominence in the twentieth century, and Carter began as a Stavinskian neo-classicist – an example is the ballet *Pocahontas* (1939) – but later wrote uncompromisingly modern music of great complexity, although in traditional forms, such as the symphony, piano concerto and string quartet.

Conlon Nancarrow (1912–97)

An American-born Mexican, Nancarrow devised music so complex that it was almost impossible to play. From 1950, his chosen method was to use a mechanical or 'player' piano. This he programmed by punching holes in a paper roll, which, when fed through the instrument, operated the keys. He was particularly interested in the effect produced by combining rhythms and melody lines in a contrapuntal way. For example, he would have one line speeding up (*accelerando*) and another simultaneously slowing down (*ritardando*). The sound of this at varying speeds is quite extraordinary, and well worth a listen.

Gyorgy Ligeti (b.1923)

In the immediate post war period (1945-9), Ligeti studied at the Budapest Academy in his native Hungary. Not surprisingly he was influenced by his compatriot Bela Bartok, and showed an early interest in the work of Schoenberg and Webern. Much of his music is characterized by the use of slow-moving blocks of sound or 'clusters'. He has produced much orchestral and chamber music, and his *Requiem* (1965) was used as background music in the film *2001: A Space Odyssey*. He has a passion for clocks and in 1962 wrote a *Poème Symphonique* for 100 metronomes.

Luigi Nono (1924–90)

Very much a serialist, Venetian born Nono was closely associated with the avant garde movement of the 1950s, and particularly with Boulez and Stockhausen. He developed the methods of Arnold Schoenberg (who in 1955 became his father-in-law), but infused his revolutionary musical ideas with a similarly radical left-wing political polemic. Nono made use of new vocal and electronic techniques in his music. He disliked the idea of the concert hall as the medium for performance and experimented with taking his music into factories to broaden his audience.

Luciano Berio (b.1925)

Berio shared Nono's connections with the European avant garde, his fascination with electronic music and different ways of employing the human voice. Many of his vocal compositions are non-verbal, but he has also set texts by Joyce, Proust and Brecht to great dramatic effect.

Hans Werner Henze (b.1926)

Although Henze's earliest compositions were in the neo-classical mould, and he later flirted with serialism, ultimately rejecting it in a lecture given at Darmstadt (a summer school which was a forum for the avant garde), in which he had the temerity to praise the concept of melody. Later, Boulez, Stockhausen and Nono publically distanced themselves from Henze's music, and he in turn declared that the **dodecaphony** had 'become a vogue and a bore'. He has returned in his later compositions to tonality and a more romantic approach, having also abandoned the revolutionary socialism that informed much of his earlier work.

Toru Takemitsu (1930–96)

Takemitsu was a Japanese composer who was happy to use western systems and instruments alongside traditional oriental materials. He employed elements as diverse as serialism, *musique concrète,* electronics and the orchestral techniques of Debussy to create his delicate tone paintings with delightful Zen titles such as *A Flock Descends into the Pentagonal Garden* for orchestra (1977), and *I Hear the Water Dreaming* for flute and orchestra (1987).

Mauricio Kagel (b.1931)

An Argentinian, Kagel worked with both music and film in Buenos Aires, before he moved to Cologne (Stockhausen's centre of operations) in 1957. However, despite his presence at the focal point of the modernist world at that time, Kagel's work betrays no obvious musical influences, drawing equally from the worlds of theatre, literature and art. This eclecticism is typified by his 1964 work *The Women* for three female singers, three actresses, a dancer, women's chorus, and electronic tapes.

Krzysztof Penderecki (b.1933)

Much interesting music emerged from Poland in the twentieth century, and Penderecki is a key figure. He studied, and later taught at the Krakow Conservatory, but received international recognition with *Threnody for the Victims of Hiroshima*, written in 1960 for a large string orchestra (a threnody is a song or speech of lamentation). This work pushes the outer limits of music according to our definitions in Chapter 02, as there are no discernible elements of melody, harmony or rhythm. The writer and broadcaster Michael Hall said of Penderecki's motivation for the piece: 'it would seem that his purpose was to make noise expressive'. This he does, to chilling emotional effect, but the question arises, where does the composer go from there? In later works, from the 1970s onwards, Penderecki adopted a tonal, neo-romantic approach. If you like modern Polish music, Witold Lutoslawski (1913–1994) is a pioneering figure and worth checking out.

Henryk Górecki (b.1933)

A compatriot and exact contemporary of Penderecki, Górecki studied for a time with Messiaen in Paris, but his earlier severely atonal techniques gave way in the Third Symphony, *Symphony of Sorrowful Songs* (1976), to a use of polyphonic forms and canons. The second movement is a setting of a prayer scratched on the wall of a Gestapo prison in Poland by an eighteen-year-old girl, and is set with a moving simplicity for soprano voice. This work achieved great popularity throughout the world, and was number six in the UK best-selling album charts in 1993! If you haven't already heard it, listen to this haunting music without delay.

The Manchester School

This was the nickname given to a group of British composers who studied at the Royal Manchester College of Music in the 1950s. They drew their inspiration from both ends of the historical spectrum: medieval music and modernism. The best known of the group are Peter Maxwell Davies (b.1934), and Harrison Birtwistle (b.1934). Listen first to Davies's *Eight Songs for a Mad King* (1969), then to some of his later work and to Birtwistle's opera, *The Mask of Orpheus* (1973–84).

Arvo Pärt (b.1935)

After an early flirtation with serialism, Pärt devised his own system, which he calls 'tintinnabuli', involving bell-like sonorities, set against simple melodies reminiscent of early church music. An Estonian, and a member of the Orthodox Church, he has taken religious themes for many of his works, since moving to Berlin in 1982. You might like to try *Beatitudes* (1990), for chorus and organ, as a starting point, then work back to the intriguingly titled *If Bach had been a bee-keeper* (1978–80) for harpsichord and chamber ensemble.

John Tavener (b.1944)

Not to be confused with John Taverner (1490–1545) – a church music composer and the subject of an opera by Peter Maxwell Davies. Tavener is an English composer who, like Pärt, is a member of the Russian Orthodox church, and most of his works have a spiritual dimension. His *Song for Athene* was performed at the funeral of Diana, Princess of Wales in 1997, but his best-known work to date is *The Protecting Veil* (1987), an evocative piece for 'cello and string orchestra, which became a best-selling album.

Extending the audience – the 'dumbing down' debate

Along with the minimalists, composers like Górecki, Pärt and Tavener have regained the audience that had been alienated by the atonal movement. However, their music has been derided for its 'simplicity', with detractors insisting that new works should be iconoclastic and present more of a challenge to the audience. I would argue that this type of music has a different kind of complexity and requires a radical shift of mindset on the part of the listener to appreciate it fully. It is too easy to dismiss music because it can be readily understood in terms of tonality. This is to ignore the integrity of the music itself and the sincerity of the composer in attempting to communicate with the audience.

Crossover

The question of sincerity in communication can become blurred when the marketing departments of large music corporations become involved. Since the early days of commercial recordings, adaptations of classical themes have been made with varying degrees of success. On the principle that 'you can't keep a good tune down', themes have been lifted from Rimski-Korsakov, Borodin, Chopin, Tchaikovsky and many others, and given a makeover to conform with the pop rhythms of the period. Past decades have seen several projects of this type. For example, the Royal Philharmonic Orchestra issued compilations of classical themes held together with a 70s' disco drumming track, called *Hooked on Classics*. Bands such as Sky featured classically trained and versatile 'session' musicians, who reworked material from the classical repertoire. Most recently, ensembles like Bond, Opera Babes, Medaeval Baebes, and the violinist Vanessa Mae have enjoyed success by re-packaging classical and operatic music with contemporary techniques and presentation borrowed from the 'pop' world. This of course is the antithesis of the authentic performance practice we discussed earlier (pages 68–9), and it may reflect unease on the part of recording company executives who are fearful of a diminishing audience for classical music.

More creative experiments in crossover have been made by jazz musicians such as the pianist Jacques Loussier who, with his jazz trio, has improvised on the works of J. S. Bach from the 1960s onwards. John Dankworth, the jazz saxophonist and composer who studied at the Royal Academy of Music, has collaborated for many years with musicians from eastern and western classical traditions. He and his wife, singer Cleo Laine, have always refused to recognize the artificial barriers dividing jazz, classical and other forms of music. Since 1969, they have organized the Wavendon Allmusic Plan from their home, where artists from all musical spheres meet to perform, teach and work on new projects.

Composers today recognize the importance of jazz and other world-wide music in a serious way. In the United Kingdom, for example, Mark-Anthony Turnage (b.1960), and Thomas Adès (b. 1971) produce orchestral music, which cannot be classified into any of the schools or styles mentioned earlier in this chapter. Imaginative instrumentalists like the percussionist Evelyn Glennie are constantly commissioning new pieces from various sources to add to their repertoire. Art is not created in isolation and the works of a composer reflect the conditions of the world in which they are created. In response to the catalclysmic events of September 11, 2001, John Adams produced *On the Transmigration of Souls*, for orchestra, chorus and tape. Meanwhile, Stockhausen, who is now an elder statesman of modernism says: 'I go on, no matter how difficult it is – I go on'. One of his later works is written for a string quartet, with each player in a separate helicopter, and the composer synchronizing the musical and mechanical sounds from his base on the ground. Musicians are happy to make use of any or all of the different tools that are available to them, including 12-note techniques, neo-romantic ideas, jazz, minimalist methods, rock and pop style electronics and computers, to express their musical ideas. The label 'classical music' is becoming more difficult to define. Should we bother? I think not. Just listen to the music.

options

In this chapter you will learn:

● where you might go from here, including suggestions of one or two directions in which you may wish to go to apply and extend your new knowledge and broaden your musical horizons.

Building a collection of recorded music

Having read this book, you should now feel equipped to make informed choices about your future musical experiences, and begin your investigation of the larger world of classical music. If you don't already, you should make full use of the broadcasting system, especially radio. The United Kingdom is well-served for classical music, with BBC Radio 3 and Classic FM, both of which run reviews of new recordings, as well as concerts, discussions and interviews. If your local library has a recorded music section, then this might be another way of getting to know unfamiliar works. There are a number of periodicals on sale featuring reviews of new recordings, like the long-established (founded in 1923) *Gramophone* magazine, which also publishes an annual *Good CD Guide*. Publications like these can be very useful, as the recording industry is extremely active in releasing a continuous flow of new performances into an ever more confusing market. I suggest you take your time, sift through all this information at your leisure, and then invest carefully in recordings on the basis of all your listening and reading.

When building your collection, begin with the music you know you like, rather than something you think you ought to like. For example, if you like Beethoven symphonies, don't jump from there to, say, the sixteenth-century madigalists, because you feel you ought to know something about them. Go for something more familiar, like Schubert or Brahms, and gradually extend your listening range. CDs, though currently the best means of reproducing music, are not cheap, and you don't want shelves full of costly mistakes that you never listen to. We all have a few gathering dust (I know I have), but let's keep them to a minimum.

Hi-fi equipment

There is a plethora of books and magazines about which type of equipment to buy. Choices abound of integrated systems or separates: amplifiers, tuners, speakers, and so on. It can be fun choosing, but the only reliable guides are your own ears, so the golden rule is: always listen before you buy. It's a good idea to take along a favourite CD, so you can compare the sound in the showroom with that produced by your current system, If you're starting from scratch, the same remarks apply, listen first, buy the best you can afford, and don't be seduced by unnecessary gadgets.

The concert scene

Recorded music is an essential part of most people's lives, and standards of reproduction are rising all the time. But a live performance is always the ultimate experience for the music lover, as we discovered in Chapter 08. So, if you have not already done so, please make arrangements to attend a concert as soon as you can. You will not regret it. If you live anywhere near a city with a resident orchestra, you could contact their 'home' venue and obtain a prospectus. All professional orchestras and major concert halls operate a mailing service (and usually a website), through which you can receive details of forthcoming events.

Concert marketing is now a very efficient operation, and you should have no trouble in keeping yourself informed. When you examine your prospectus, you will see that the bulk of the repertoire comes from the period between 1750 and the early 1900s, with at least one famous composer per concert. Early music concerts are rare, to be given by specialist groups, and even Baroque masters like Bach and Handel are perhaps not heard as often as they should be. However, these conditions are constantly changing, as managements adapt to prevailing tastes.

Most programmes are thoughtfully designed, often with a thematic link of some sort to connect the pieces. As you will remember from Chapter 14, some twentieth-century pieces are still considered 'difficult', and do not always make popular concert items. It is fairly standard practice for programmers to sandwich these works in between more popular items, so that the audience is more or less compelled to sample them, and the pieces receive a fair hearing. The favourite spot is at the end of the first half of the concert, before the interval. This way, if the first piece is popular, you have a captive audience for the second, followed by refreshments, and a major work in the second half to send the customers away happy.

The symphony orchestra is an expensive beast, and a manager naturally wants to fill the hall as often as possible with paying customers, and the easiest way to do that is by sticking to the 'safe' programmes with proven popularity. But, most orchestras do commission new works on a regular basis, investing some revenue in the music of the future. Sponsorship is another means of generating funds, persuading wealthy companies to underwrite concerts. The nature of the programmes sponsored depends upon the extent of influence the sponsor has over the musical content. The system seems to work in the United States, where this method of funding is the norm, but in the United Kingdom financial support may come from a variety of sources, such as local government, central government via the Arts Council, the European Union, various trusts and individual donations. One thing is certain, professional orchestras could not survive without subsidies of one sort or another.

Meeting people

Listening to music doesn't have to be a solitary occupation. Most towns have a musical society of one sort or another. Your local college may run evening classes on various aspects of music. If you can play an instrument, or would like to learn, there are many amateur orchestras and bands who are always on the lookout for new members, and local teachers who will provide tuition. Finally, if you would really like to take the bull by the horns and study music full time, there are routes which can take you through to music college or university. Ask at your local college for details. The world of music is wide and welcoming – happy listening!

glossary

Abbreviations

It. = Italian, Fr. = French, Ger. = German, Gr. = Greek, Lat. = Latin, n. = noun.

accompaniment Secondary part, supporting a more important theme or themes.

adagio (It. *'at ease'*) Slow tempo often used for slow symphonic movements. Title of well-known pieces by Albinoni (1671–1750) and Samuel Barber (1910–81).

aleatory Music in which there are elements of chance or opportunities for random occurrences in performance. Particularly associated with John Cage, but also employed by Boulez, Stockhausen and others.

allegretto Moderately quick tempo, slower than **allegro** (see below).

allegro (It. *'bright'*, *'lively'*) Quick tempo; **allegro molto** is very quick tempo.

allemande 1) One of the four dances which comprised the Suite in the 17th and 18th centuries. Slow tempo in duple time; 2) Lively rustic dance in triple time.

andante (It. *'moving'*) Fairly slow tempo, walking pace.

aria (It. *'air'*) Solo song, especially in operatic performances.

arpeggio (It. *harp-like*) A 'spread' chord, the notes played one after the other.

atonal (n. **atonality**) Music which is not based on a tonal system (see **tonality**).

avant garde (Fr. 'vanguard') In music, this term has come to represent the work of those European composers who were in the forefront of innovation in the decades following the Second World War (1945 to around 1970) (see also **modernism**).

ballade (Fr. *'ballad'*) Musical composition based on a narrative, especially for piano.

basso continuo See **continuo**.

bel canto (It. *'beautiful song'*) Operatic singing in the Italian style, particularly appropriate to the works of 19th-century composers.

binary form A piece of music in two sections, usually with both sections repeated (see also **ternary form**).

cadence A melodic or harmonic phrase to end a section of a composition. There are several distinct types of cadence, the most common (and final) being the 'perfect cadence', involving a fall from **dominant** to **tonic**.

cadenza An unaccompanied passage in a virtuoso style, usually at the end of the first movement of a concerto, utilizing the material in that movement.

canon A piece in which two or more parts follow one another at a fixed distance, in strict imitation.

cantata (It. *'sung'*) A vocal work, similar to opera, but not staged. Soloists, chorus and orchestra were common from 18th century onwards. Subject matter is generally, but not always religious.

canzona (It. *'song'*, Fr. *chanson*) A vocal piece with instrumental accompaniment, or an instrumental piece in a vocal style.

celesta A keyboard instrument, the keys operating hammers which strike metal bars, producing a tinkling sound not unlike the glockenspiel (see page 87), but rather lighter. Invented in 1886, the instrument was first used by Tchaikovsky in the Dance of the Sugar Plum Fairy, from the ballet *Nutcracker*.

chaconne See **passacaglia**.

chamber music Literally, music to be performed in a house, rather than a church, theatre or concert hall. In practice, the term is used to describe small-scale instrumental music, written for two or more instruments, with one instrument to a part.

chorale A hymn tune of the German Lutheran Church. Often used as a basis for free development in organ pieces (**chorale prelude** and **chorale fantasia**), or **cantatas**, many of which were composed by Bach.

chord Three or more different notes sounded together (see also **harmony**).

chromatic (Gr. '*coloured*') In tonal music, notes or chords outside the framework of the controlling scale or key.

coda (It. '*tail*') A passage of varying length at the end of a work, or movement within a longer work, which brings the piece to its conclusion.

codetta A shorter version of the above, which usually appears within a piece, for example at the end of the exposition in sonata form.

concert A public performance of music by more than two players that does not involve theatrical staging (see also **recital**).

concertino 1) In the 17th and 18th centuries **concerto grosso**, the name given to the group of solo instruments; 2) A shorter version of the **concerto**, used in the 19th century by composers like Weber.

concerto From the 18th century, a work for one or more solo instruments, with orchestral accompaniment. Before that time, the word was used to describe various types of vocal and instrumental ensemble.

continuo or **basso continuo** An improvised (usually keyboard) accompaniment, common in the 17th and 18th centuries. A single bass line was written, with a numerical indication of the harmony the accompanist was to use (figured bass).

counterpoint The mixing of two or more independent melodic lines within a harmonic context.

contrapuntal The adjective of **counterpoint**.

courante (Fr. '*running*') A lively dance in triple time. Part of the dance suite of the 17th and 18th centuries.

crescendo (It. '*increasing*') A gradual increase in volume.

da capo (It. '*from the head*') An indication for the performer to go back to the beginning of the piece. A da capo aria is one in which the final section (of three) is a repeat of the first, usually with improvised vocal embellishments.

descant From Latin *discantus*, meaning '*different song*'. The precise meaning changes with the period, but generally, this refers to a separate vocal line above the other parts in choral music.

development The investigation of the musical potential of given material, by various means. The section of a symphonic movement in sonata form where this occurs.

diatonic In tonal music, the notes of the major and minor scales, and chords built upon them.

diminuendo (It. '*diminishing*') A gradual decrease in volume.

dodecaphonic (n. **dodecaphony**) Music composed on the 12-note principle devised by Arnold Schoenberg.

dominant In tonal music, the name given to the fifth degree of the major or minor scale, or the chord built upon it. Closely related to the **tonic**, the dominant and tonic chords are often heard at the end of a piece, providing a final 'full stop'. The formal term for this type of ending is 'perfect cadence'. (See also **cadence**.)

dynamics The extent of, and variations in, loudness and softness in music. The same term refers both to performance and to written notation.

ensemble (Fr. '*together*') A group of singers or instrumentalists.

entr'acte (Fr.) Music played between the acts in a theatrical performance.

étude (Fr. '*study*') A piece intended to produce improvements in playing technique. In the hands of Chopin, however, the form was elevated beyond mere mechanical practice to works of great artistic merit.

fantasia (It. '*fantasy*' or '*fancy*') A piece in which there are no formal constraints on the composer (or player if improving). **Free fantasia** is an alternative name for the development section of a sonata-form movement.

finale   The final movement or section of a large-scale work, like a symphony, concerto, opera, etc.

form   a term used to describe the structure of any given piece. See **binary form, ternary form, sonata form**.

fugato   A fugal section within a work which is not itelf a **fugue** (see next entry).

fugue   (It. '*flight*') A type of composition in which two or more parts enter individually, with the same subject matter, which is then developed contrapuntally.

galant   (Fr. '*courteous*') Style of music that was stately, imposing and dignified in the 18th century.

galliard   A merry dance in triple time, popular in the 16th and 17th centuries, when it was often alternated with the **pavane**.

gigue   (It. '*jig*') A lively dance, the final dance of the four commonly found in dance suite of the 17th and 18th centuries.

glissando (-i)   (from Fr. *glisser*, 'to slide') A musical slur from low to high notes or vice versa, most easily achieved on unfretted stringed instruments, the harp and the trombone, the latter being used in traditional jazz for comic effect.

harmonics   Overtones of a musical note.

harmony   In tonal music, the system of chordal movement, combination and juxtaposition, based on the diatonic scales and keys. Prior to the 17th century, the word simply referred to pleasing musical sounds.

idée fixe   (Fr. '*fixed idea*') A term used by Berlioz to describe a theme which represents an idea or character, and recurs in various forms throughout a piece.

interval   The difference in pitch between any two notes, normally named after the degrees of the diatonic scale, e.g. 4th, 5th and so on. The best-known interval, and the easiest to identify, is the octave, spanning the full eight notes of the scale.

key   A term which defines the basic tonality of a piece, where the controlling system of major and minor scales, and related chords, must begin and end.

Ländler   An Austrian dance in slow triple time, said to be a forerunner of the waltz. Ländler-style movements can be found in the works of Austrian and German composers from Haydn to Mahler.

legato   (It. '*bound*') Played with notes smoothly connected. The opposite of **staccato**.

Leitmotiv   (Ger. '*leading theme*') A term used by Wagner to describe recurring themes, which represent characters, ideas or objects in his operas.

libretto (-i)   (It. '*little book*') The text of an opera or oratorio.

Lieder   (Ger. '*songs*') This term is now used specifically to describe German Romantic songs from Schubert to Strauss, with expressive piano accompaniment.

madrigal   A secular unaccompanied vocal composition, making much use of **counterpoint**, which originated in fourteenth-century Italy. An English madrigal school developed in the second half of the sixteenth century.

masque   In the 16th and 17th century in England, a dramatic entertainment involving pantomime, dancing and song.

mazurka   A Polish folk dance in quick triple time, often with the second beat accented. Chopin wrote over 50 pieces in this form.

melody   A series of musical sounds which form a recognizable shape.

metronome   A machine which produces a regular and measured beat. Patented by Maelzel in 1816.

microtones   Intervals of less than a semitone, that is, smaller than the sharps and flats that lie in between some of the degrees of the scale. Several 20th-century composers have made use of microtones.

minimalism   A style which evolved in the 1960s, largely of American origin, involving the repetition of short melodic figures over static harmony, often developing considerable rhythmic complexity.

minuet   (Ger.: **Menuett**, It.: **menuetto**) A French dance in moderate triple time, often appearing in the dance suite of the 17th and 18th centuries. The minuet also appeared as a movement in sonatas, symphonies and quartets before Beethoven.

modernism   A term generally applied to the music of those composers who, after the First World War (1918), adopted radical new techniques; principally, but not exclusively, those of atonality (*see also* **postmodernism**).

modes Scales, or series of notes in use from medieval times, until the advent of the tonal system, with its major and minor scales (themselves derived from earlier modes) took over at the end of the 17th century. Modes are also used by some jazz musicians as a basis for improvisation.

modulation In tonal music, the practice of moving from key to key in a logical progression. Much used in the development sections of sonata-form movements.

motet An unaccompanied vocal piece based on a sacred text, developed from plainsong, but normally contrapuntal.

motif Synonymous with **theme**, a melodic idea, or subject, which is announced, developed and often transformed, during the course of a piece.

movement A substantial section of a larger piece, such as a symphony, concerto, etc., which has some degree of independence from other sections, but from the 19th century there have often been thematic links between them. In concert performances, movements are usually (but not always) separated by a short break (without applause).

nocturne (night-piece) Short, lyrical piece of music, usually for piano.

obbligato (It. '*obligatory*') 1) In Baroque music, a part for a solo instrument, with a separate melodic line, which is added to the accompaniment of an aria; 2) The term has since been used to describe an optional extra part, a fact which can cause some confusion.

opus (Lat. '*work*') Often shortened to Op., a method used by composers and their publishers for cataloguing their works. Unfortunately, they cannot be relied upon to reflect accurately the order of composition.

oratorio (It. 'Oratory', Lit. place in Rome where musical services were held) Dramatic, unstaged musical composition for soloists, chorus and orchestra based on a religious theme.

orchestration The art of translating musical ideas into orchestral terms.

ostinato A melodic or rhythmic pattern which is repeated through a significant portion of a piece. A bass ostinato is also known as a **ground bass**.

overture An introductory piece, usually in one movement, played before an opera, oratorio or theatrical work, or a **concert overture**, which is a free-standing work, often played at the beginning of a concert.

partita 1) Up to the 17th century, a theme with variations; 2) Later used, particularly by Bach, as another word for 'suite'.

passacaglia Often linked with the **chaconne**, which is almost identical. From the 17th century, a slow dance in triple time, with variations, over a ground bass. The form was revived by Brahms, in the finale of his Symphony No. 4, and has been taken up by several 20th-century composers.

pavane A slow dance in duple time, dating from the 16th century, when it was often linked with the **galliard**.

pizzicato (It. '*plucked*') An instruction to string players to pluck the strings with the fingers, rather than to use the bow.

Polonaise Polish march-like dance in three-four time; Chopin wrote many pieces in this style.

polyphony (Gr. '*many sounds*') Music which is characterized by the interweaving of separate melodic strands, rather than chord-based harmony.

polytonality The combination of two or more different keys. If the practice is restricted to two keys, the result is **bitonality**. These techniques were not seriously used until the 20th century, when they were taken up by Stravinsky, Bartok and Holst, among others.

postmodernism This is not as common a term in musical criticism as in the worlds of literature and the visual arts, but it can be used to describe contemporary music (since around 1970) that employs tonal methods of composition.

recital A public performance of music for one or two players, with or without an accompaniment.

recitative In opera and oratorio, a type of singing which retains many of the inflections and rhythms of speech. Usually accompanied by **continuo**.

rhythm The patterns of music determined according to time.

ricercare (It. '*to seek out*') The contrapuntal 'working out' of a theme or set of themes, a favourite form of 16th- and 17th-century organist-composers.

ripieno (It. '*full*') In the Baroque concerto grosso, the orchestral body, as opposed to the concertino group of solo instruments.

sarabande A dance in slow triple time. One of the four basic dances constituting the 17th- and 18th-century dance suite.

scale A stepwise progression of notes, ascending or descending, arranged according to the sytem of major or minor tonality.

scherzo (It. '*joke*') A lively movement, developed from the **minuet**, with a contrasting middle section.

score A complete written orchestration, with all the parts set out separately on the page. The conventional form is (in descending vertical order) woodwind, brass, percussion and strings, with solo or keyboard instruments and/or voices appearing between the percussion and strings.

serialism A strict application, or development of the 12-note principle, as set out by Schoenberg.

Singspiel (Ger. '*sing-play*') German comic opera with spoken dialogue.

sonata (from It. *sonare*, 'to sound') 1) Before c.1750 a composition for solo instrument or instruments plus continuo; 2) After c.1750, a work for solo keyboard instrument, or solo instrument with piano accompaniment.

sonata form An extension of the ternary idea, which became the norm for the first movement and sometimes the finale in the orchestral and chamber music of the Classical and Romantic periods. See Chapter 04.

staccato (It. '*detached*') Played with each note clearly separated.

string quartet An ensemble of two violins, viola and cello, and the music written for such a group.

suite 1) In the 17th and 18th centuries, a set of movements based on dance-forms, all in the same key; 2) More recently, a work in several movements, often taken from incidental or ballet music, or with a linking idea (e.g. Holst's suite, *The Planets*).

symphony 1) Before c.1750, used to describe music of various kinds, usually instrumental; 2) After c.1750, a work similar in form to the **sonata**, but written for full orchestra.

tempo (It. '*time*') The speed or pace at which a composition is performed. This is specified by the composer, either approximately (e.g. **adagio**, **allegro**, etc.) or precisely by indicating a **metronome** mark. In either case, the conductor is assumed to have some interpretative influence in setting the tempo.

ternary form A piece of music in three sections with the first and last sections contrasting with the second section (see also **binary form**).

theme A musical idea, often used as the basis for development (see also **motif**).

timbre Tone quality or colour.

toccata (It. from **toccare** '*to touch*') An elaborate keyboard piece, designed to display the technique of the performer. Popular with Baroque organists, often followed by a fugue.

tonal (n. **tonality**) That type of music which is composed according to the system of diatonic major and minor scales, and the chords derived from them.

tonic The fundamental note of a diatonic scale, which prescribes the key of a piece based upon it.

tremolo, tremolando Rapid reiteration of a single note, most frequently used on stringed instruments to add to dramatic tension.

twelve-note (US: **twelve-tone**) **composition** A system devised by Schoenberg in which all 12 notes within the span of an octave are played in a predetermined order, which dictates both melody and harmony. There is no controlling or 'key' -note, so the music is therefore **atonal.**

vibrato A method of sustaining and enriching the quality of a note on stringed and wind instruments, and in singing, by adding tiny pulsations to the pitch of the note.

virtuoso A solo instrumental performer of exceptional skill and artistry.

taking it further

Further reading

Atkins, Harold, and Newman, Archie *Beecham Stories* (Warner Books, first published 1978)
Just for fun, anecdotes about the great conductor and wit.

Berlioz, Hector *Memoirs* (Gollancz, 1969)
A fascinating insight into the mind of this extraordinary Romantic.

Bukofzer, Manfred F. *Music in the Baroque Era* (Dent, 1947)
Still the last word on Baroque style.

Cooper, M. (ed.) *New Oxford History of Music*, 10 vols. (Oxford University Press, 1974)

Fenby, Eric *Delius as I knew Him* (Icon Books 1936, revised 1966)

Griffiths, Paul *Modern Music: A Concise History* (Thames and Hudson, 1994)
An illustrated guide to the world of twentieth-century music.

Grout and Palisca *A History of Western Music* 6th Edition (Norton, 2001)
A solid, up-to-date history in one volume.

Kernfield, Barry (ed.) *The New Grove Dictionary of Jazz* (Macmillan, 1994)
Scholarly single-volume dictionary, covering all aspects of this exciting music.

Landon, H. C. R., and Mitchell, D. (Eds.) *The Mozart Companion* (Faber, 1965)
Musiologist H. C. Robbins Landon has written many books about composers such as Haydn (3 vol. biography), Mozart, Handel and Vivaldi. His work is the product of thorough research, and is always eminently readable.

Lang, P. H. *Music in Western Civilization* (Norton, 1997, first published 1941)

Nicholas, Jeremy *Classic FM Good Music Guide* (1999) The book contains descriptions of 1,000 pieces of classical music, and recommends appropriate pieces for different occasions and moods.

Richer, Margaret *Teach Yourself Music Theory* (Hodder & Stoughton, 2003)
A good introduction to the technicalities of music.

Rosen, Charles *The Classical Style* (Norton, 1997)
Excellent, but requires some technical knowledge.

Sadie, Julie Anne *The New Grove Dictionary of Women Composers* (Macmillan, 1994)
This essential book takes an important step towards correcting a male bias, which has perpetuated throughout the history of music.

Sadie, Stanley (ed.) *The New Grove Dictionary of Music and Musicians*, 29 vols, Macmillan (2001)
The ultimate reference book, now available on line.

Sadie, Stanley (ed.) *The New Grove Concise Dictionary of Music* (Macmillan, 1988)
An affordable single-volume reference book, bearing the distinguished name of George Grove.

Scholes, Percy A. (ed.) *The Oxford Companion of Music* (OUP, first published 1938 but constantly updated).

The Gramophone Classical Good CD Guide
  A mine of information, with masses of articles from well-known critics. Updated yearly.

The Master Musicians Series (Oxford University Press)
  Biographical studies of all major composers and their works. Utterly reliable.

Websites

www.classical.net
A large and comprehensive site, giving information on composers and their works, reviews and articles, books and scores, plus dozens of useful links.

www.classicallink.net
Lots of links, also articles and interviews. Music samples and downloads are available to subscribers.

www.britishclassicalmusic.com
Very informative site, specializing in British music.

www.gramophone.co.uk
The website belonging to the famous magazine, containing articles and reviews.

www.ambache.co.uk/wIndex.htm
Under the title 'Women of Note' you will find 36 biographies (with musical examples) of women composers and performers, including Fanny Mendelssohn, Clara Schumann, and Germaine Tailleferre (1892–1983, one of *Les Six*, see page 88). Elsewhere on the site there are discussions and articles about women composers, all presented by the pianist and lecturer, Diana Ambache.

www.bbc.co.uk/music/classical/index.shtml

This is the classical music section of the huge BBC site, giving many articles, information about artists, and the latest broadcasting news.

There are also many commercial sites through which you can buy CDs, sheet music, instruments, etc., as well as sites specializing in information about individual composers and performers. Just put the appropriate name into your search engine, and surf the net!